CAMBRIDGE
Cambridge Chinese
Workbook 1
for Beginners

Cambridge Chinese Workbook 1 was written in accompaniment to *Cambridge Chinese Textbook 1*. The workbook has been written for students studying the language as a beginner. The contents of this workbook are fully aligned to the six units of the textbook which will enable the student to revise and practise the fundamental basics of Mandarin Chinese.

This workbook tests the students' understanding in terms of pinyin, tones and Chinese characters. There are also useful pointers and grammar clues to remind the students and help them as they make their way through the book. Similiar to Textbook 1, the explanations and exercises are clearly and attractively laid out, making it easy for the students to relate to the topics previously learnt and then apply them in the workbook.

Not only does this workbook allow students to revise the language learnt in the lessons, but it also tests them on Chinese cultural topics that they would have previously learnt. In addition, there are many exercises that prompt students to use resources around them to answer the workbook's questions. It is this cultural aspect and realistic approach to testing a language, along with the clear grammatical layout, that make this workbook stand apart from others. Good luck!

Unit 1

UNIT 1 - HELLO!

First words in Chinese

Exercise 1.1 – Do you remember these words?
Look at the words below and identify the correct Chinese translations for the English words on the left. We have completed number one for you.

1. hello	a. 谢谢　xièxie
2. goodbye	b. 好　　hǎo
3. thank you	c. 老师　lǎoshī
4. teacher	d. 你好　nǐ hǎo
5. good	e. 再见　zàijiàn

Exercise 1.2 – Which tone is that?
For each of the words that have no tone annotation shown, draw a line from the correct tone to the correct letter in the word. We have completed number one for you.

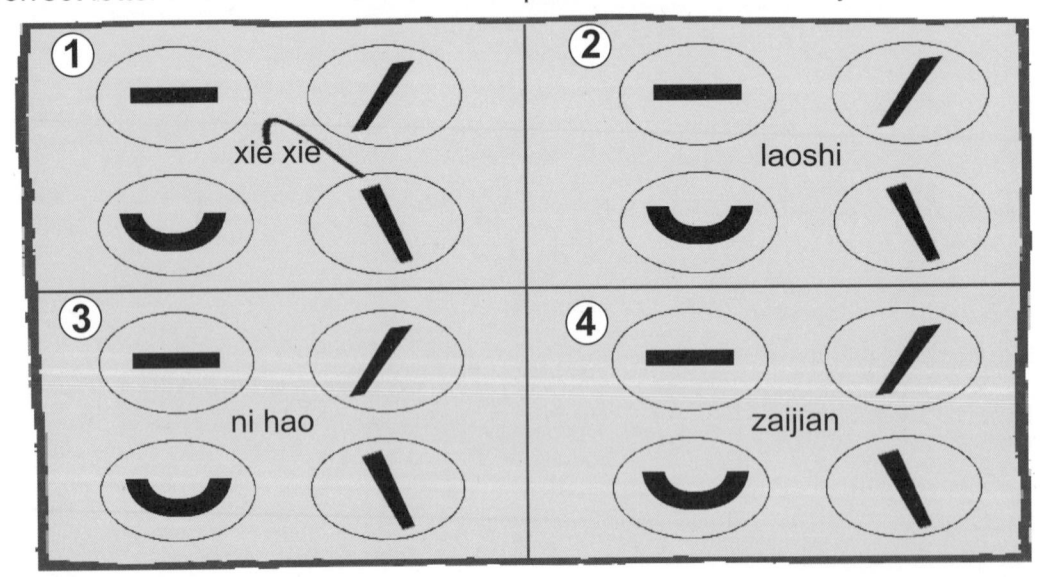

① xie xie

② laoshi

③ ni hao

④ zaijian

Exercise 1.3 – Fill in the blanks
Look at the English questions and then write the appropriate answer in Chinese in the spaces provided. We have completed an example for you.

e.g. How would you say 'hello' in Chinese?   Nǐ hǎo

1. How would you say 'goodbye' in Chinese?   _____

2. How would you say 'you' in Chinese?   _____

3. How would you say 'thank you' in Chinese?   _____

4. How would you say 'teacher' in Chinese?   _____

Unit 1

Saying 'hello' more formally in Chinese

您好 Nín hǎo = How are you?

Similar to the French 'vous' and the Spanish 'usted', there is a polite form of 'you' in Chinese which is **nín**. So when you need to be polite or when talking to an older person or someone in a position of authority, say **nín hǎo**.

Exercise 1.4 – Formal or informal?
Look at the names of the people on the left below and decide whether you should address the relevant person as either nǐ hǎo or nín hǎo. We have completed an example for you.

e.g. policeman _____Nín hǎo_____

1. fellow student _____
2. mum _____
3. your teacher _____
4. dad _____
5. headmaster _____

How to greet people in Chinese?

你好吗？ Nǐ hǎo ma? = How are you?
我很好。 Wǒ hěn hǎo. = I am very well.
…你呢。 … nǐ ne? = …and you?

Exercise 1.5 – Fill in the gaps
Look at the two short dialogues below and fill in the gaps. Clue: the words are based on the new 'greetings words' that you have just reviewed above. We have completed the first one for you.

1
Míngming: Nǐ ___hǎo___.
Mǐn: _____ hǎo.
Míngming: Nǐ hǎo _____?
Mǐn: _____ _____ hǎo, _____ ne?
Míngming: Wǒ hěn _____, _____xie.
Mǐn: Zài_____.
Míngming: Zàijiàn.

2
Guóyīng: _____ hǎo.
Mǎlì: Nǐ _____.
Guóyīng: _____ _____ ma?
Mǎlì: Wǒ _____ hǎo, nǐ _____?
Guóyīng: _____ _____ hǎo, xiè _____.
Mǎlì: Zài_____.
Guóyīng: _____.

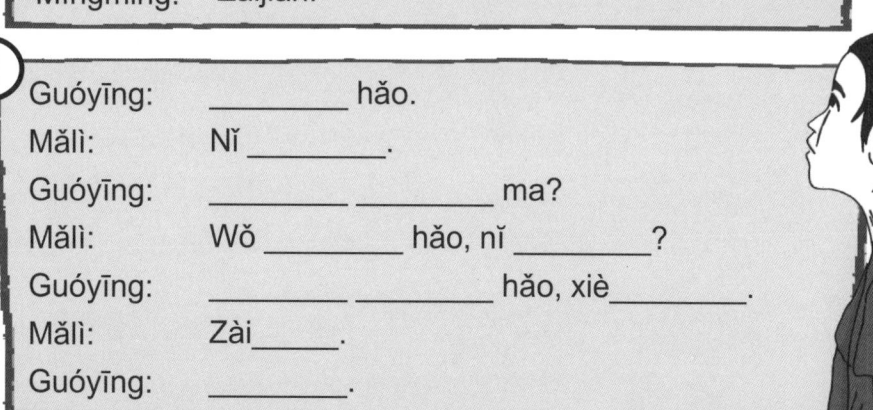

3 sān 三

Unit 1

How to apologise in Chinese?

对不起   Duìbuqǐ   =   Sorry   课本

Exercise 1.6 - Let's play 3-in-a-row!
You will find the three words that make up **duìbuqǐ** - **duì, bu** and **qǐ** - randomly placed in the grid below. Find as many examples of '3 in a row' as you can, making sure that you pick the <u>words with the correct tones</u>. We have completed an example for you.

duì	bú	qǐ	qí
bu	qí	bu	bú
qǐ	bu	duì	qǐ
duī	qī	bu	bu
bu	duǐ	duì	dui
qí	bu	qi	qí
qǐ	qǐ	bu	duì

The 'A' sounds in the four tones

The four tones in Chinese are numbered 1st, 2nd, 3rd, and 4th. Here are some examples of words that use each tone:

1st tone example:	mā	=	mum
2nd tone example:	chá	=	tea
3rd tone example:	mǎ	=	horse
4th tone example:	dà	=	big

课本

Exercise 1.7 - Choose the correct tone for these 'a' sounds
Below you will find four lists of the above words. Fill in the gaps with the corresponding words in Chinese ensuring you remember the correct tones. We have completed a few words for you.

1. tea   tea   mum   horse   mum   big   mum
    <u>chá</u>   <u>chá</u>   <u>mā</u>   ___   ___   ___   ___

2. mum   mum   big   tea   mum   horse   big
    ___   ___   ___   ___   ___   ___   ___

3. big   big   big   horse   horse   tea   horse
    ___   ___   ___   ___   ___   ___   ___

Exercise 1.8 - Recognising the 4 different tones
Choosing either 1st, 2nd 3rd or 4th tone as the answer, look at the words below and circle the correct tones. Please note: '-' means <u>no</u> tone. We have completed an example for you.

e.g.	nǐ hǎo	(3rd & 3rd)	4th & -	2nd & 3rd
1.	lǎoshī	2nd & 4th	1st & 2nd	3rd & 1st
2.	xièxie	4th & -	2nd & -	3rd & -
3.	hěn hǎo	1st & 1st	3rd & 3rd	4th & 4th
4.	nǐ ne	3rd & -	4th & -	1st & -

4 sì 四

Unit 1

Getting used to Chinese characters

Exercise 1.9 – Match the Chinese characters
Look at each of the Chinese character grids below and circle all instances of the character that you are being asked to locate. We have completed the first grid for you.

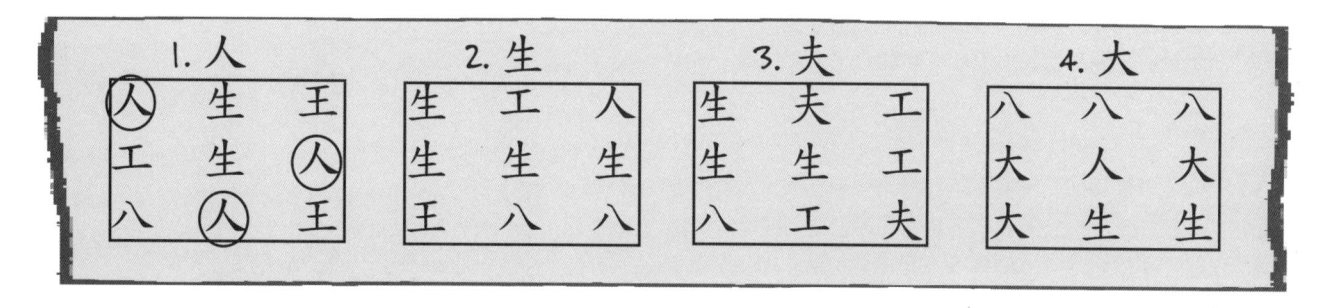

1. 人

八	生	王
工	生	人
八	人	王

2. 生

生	工	人
生	生	生
王	八	八

3. 夫

生	夫	工
生	生	工
八	工	夫

4. 大

八	八	八
大	人	大
大	生	生

Exercise 1.10 – Getting used to writing Chinese characters
Trace over the grey lines to complete the Chinese characters. Complete each Chinese character four times. Please note that the lines in the grid are there to help you with the spacing and the general presentation of each character. We have completed the first character for you.

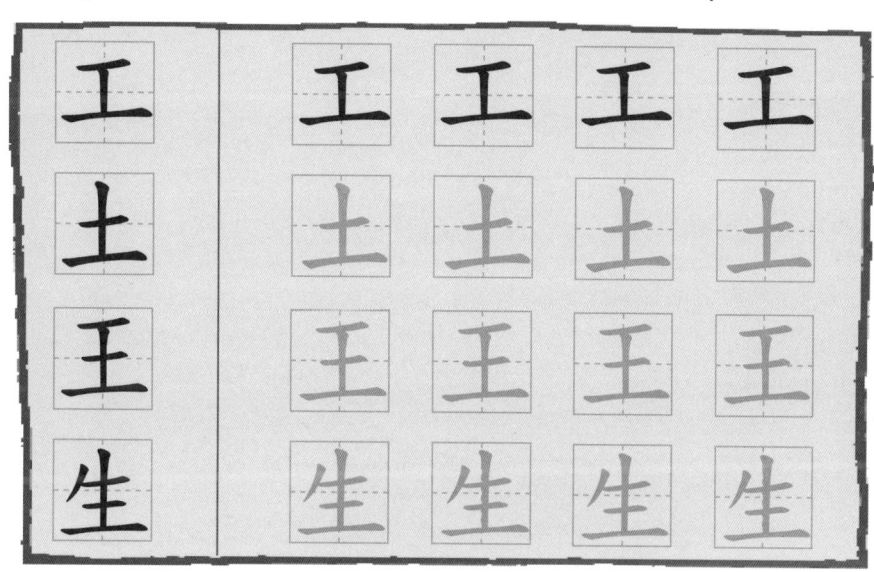

The Origins of Chinese Characters

Exercise 1.11 – Match the Chinese characters   山 目 田 火 木
In the grid below you must circle all the occurrences of <u>three matching characters in a line.</u> The answers can be in any direction! We have completed an example for you.

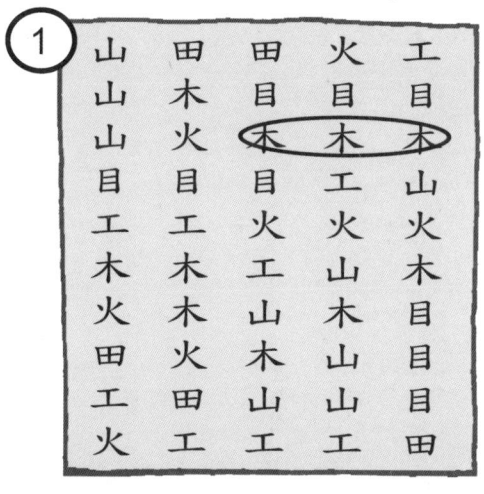

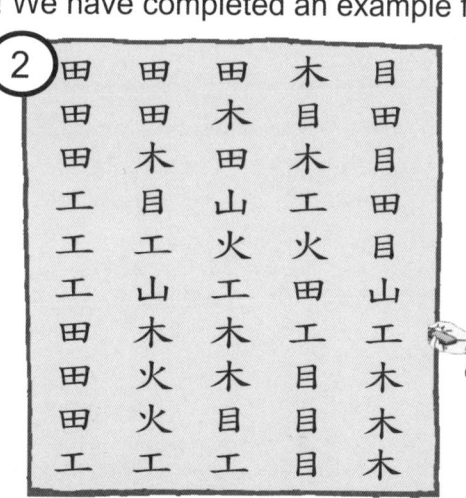

①
山	田	田	火	工
山	木	目	目	目
山	火	木	木	木
目	目	目	工	山
工	工	火	火	火
木	木	工	山	木
火	木	山	木	目
田	火	木	山	目
工	田	山	山	目
火	工	工	工	田

②
田	田	田	木	目
田	田	木	目	田
田	木	木	木	目
工	目	山	工	田
工	工	火	火	目
工	山	工	田	山
田	木	木	工	工
田	火	木	目	木
田	火	目	目	木
工	工	工	目	木

5 wǔ 五

Unit 1

Exercise 1.12 – Understanding stroke order

Chinese characters have to be written using the correct stroke order. First trace over the grey strokes and then complete the <u>full</u> character <u>3 times</u> in the empty boxes. We have completed the first character for you. Note: you will hopefully recognise 王 from page 5.

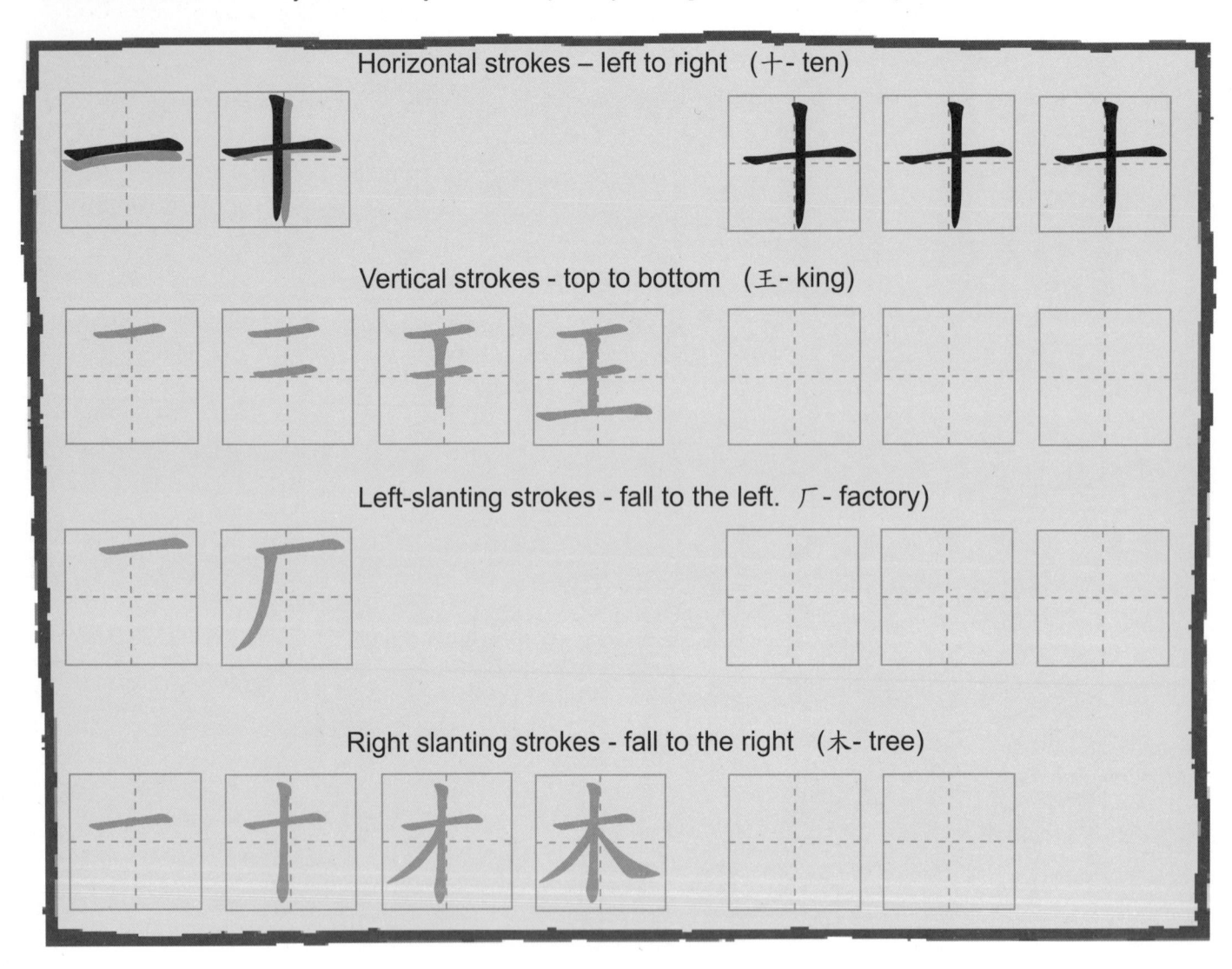

Horizontal strokes – left to right (十 - ten)

Vertical strokes - top to bottom (王 - king)

Left-slanting strokes - fall to the left. 厂 - factory)

Right slanting strokes - fall to the right (木 - tree)

How to count 1-5 in Chinese

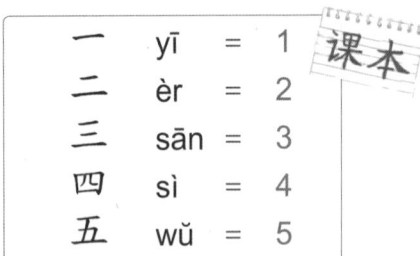

一	yī	=	1
二	èr	=	2
三	sān	=	3
四	sì	=	4
五	wǔ	=	5

课本

12345

Exercise 1.13 - Let's play 'link'!

Link the English numbers to the Chinese pinyin and vice versa. We have completed the link between 2 and **èr** for you in the first box.

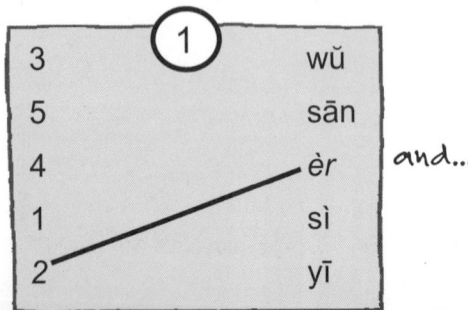

1

3	wǔ
5	sān
4	èr
1	sì
2	yī

and...

2

èr	four
sì	one
yī	five
wǔ	two
sān	three

and...

3

sì	one
yī	three
wǔ	two
sān	four
èr	five

6 liù 六

Unit 1

Writing the Chinese characters for 1-5

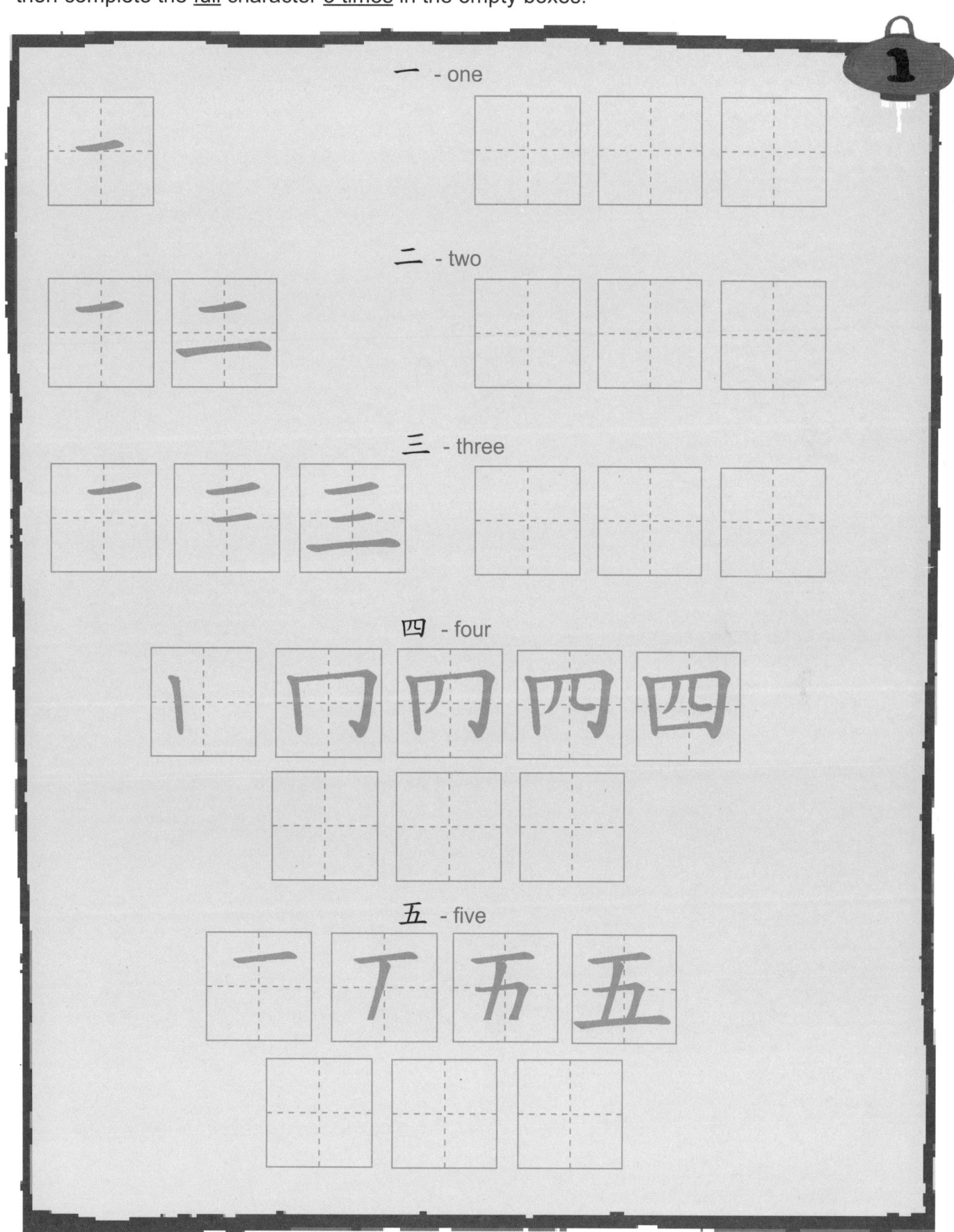

Exercise 1.14 - Writing Chinese numbers
Practise writing the Chinese characters for numbers 1–5. First trace over the grey strokes and then complete the <u>full</u> character <u>3 times</u> in the empty boxes.

一 - one

二 - two

三 - three

四 - four

五 - five

7 qī 七

Unit 1

Exercise 1.15 - Chinese numbers using characters
Link the Chinese characters on the left to the pinyin in the middle and then make the link to the correct number of bags on the right. We have completed number one for you.

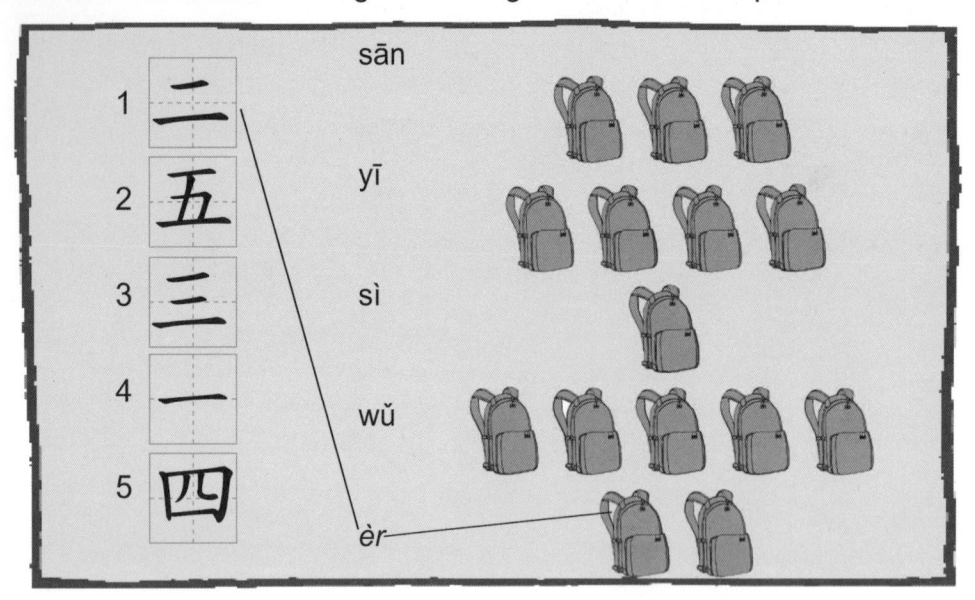

1	二	sān
2	五	yī
3	三	sì
4	一	wǔ
5	四	èr

Exercise 1.16 - Chinese Maths
Read the English questions below and write the answers using Chinese characters in the boxes provided. We have completed an example for you.

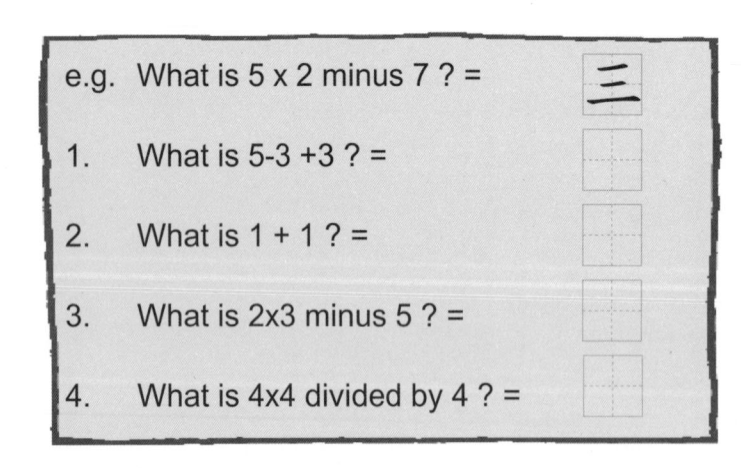

e.g. What is 5 x 2 minus 7 ? = 三

1. What is 5-3 +3 ? =
2. What is 1 + 1 ? =
3. What is 2x3 minus 5 ? =
4. What is 4x4 divided by 4 ? =

Exercise 1.17 - More Chinese Maths
Below are some maths questions using Chinese characters instead of English numbers. Work out the answer and write the number using characters. We have completed an example for you.

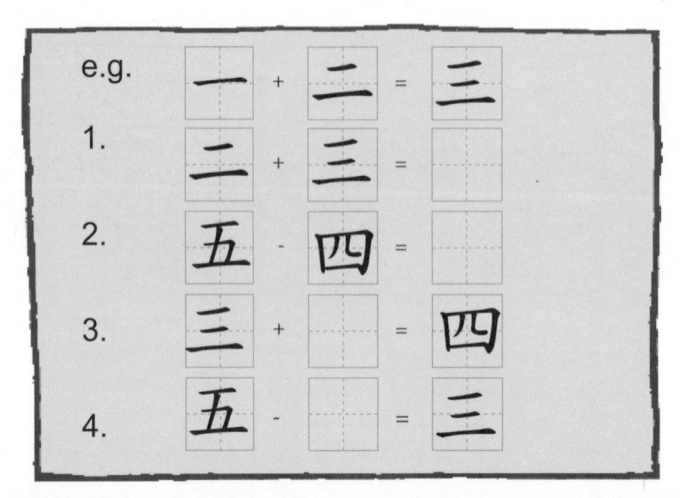

e.g. 一 + 二 = 三

1. 二 + 三 =
2. 五 - 四 =
3. 三 + ___ = 四
4. 五 - ___ = 三

8 bā 八

Some important facts about China

Exercise 1.18 - What do you know about China?
What do you remember from Unit 1? Rely on your memory or use the internet to choose the correct answers below! Tick the correct box. We have completed an example for you.

e.g. Which of the following cities lies at the mouth of the Yangtze?

   a) Shanghai ☑
   b) Beijing ☐
   c) Hong Kong ☐

1. How many people live in China?

   a) 900,000,000 ☐
   b) 1.1 billion ☐
   c) 1.9 billion ☐
   d) 1.4 billion ☐

2. Which famous Beijing landmark is called the 'Gate of Heavenly Peace'?

   _____

3. In Mandarin, Hong Kong is pronounced **Xiāng Gǎng**. How would you translate it into English?

   _____

4. What year did the British Government return Hong Kong to China?

   a) 1897 ☐
   b) 1997 ☐
   c) 2007 ☐
   d) 1977 ☐

Unit 2

UNIT 2 - ABOUT ME

Numbers 6-10

Exercise 2.1 - Word match
Link the English numbers to the Chinese pinyin. Look at the words and find the translations for 6-10 in Chinese! Complete both exercises. We have completed the link between 6 and **liù** for you!

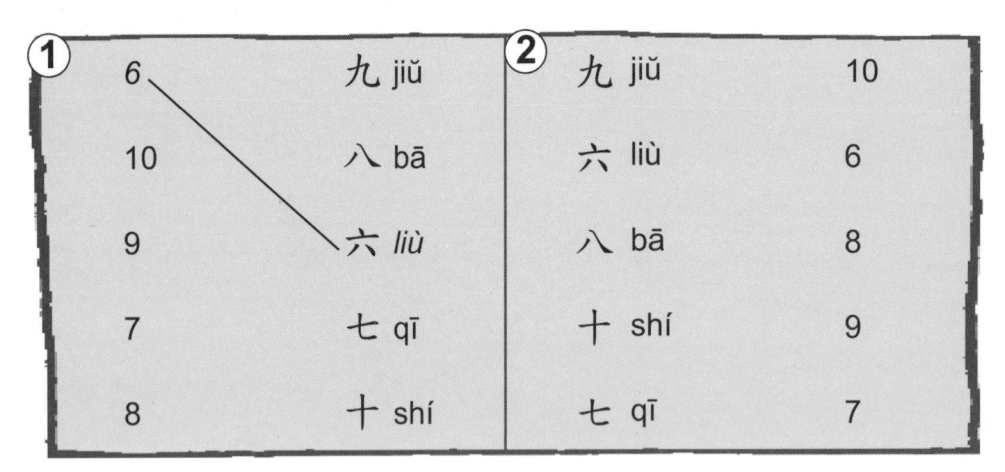

**① **
6	九 jiǔ	
10	八 bā	
9	六 liù	
7	七 qī	
8	十 shí	

**② **
九 jiǔ	10	
六 liù	6	
八 bā	8	
十 shí	9	
七 qī	7	

Exercise 2.2 - It's amazing! - Reviewing numbers 1-10 in Chinese
For each of the mazes below trace a path from start to finish. Which numbers do you pass on the way? Once you reach the finish, look back at all the numbers that the path passes through and write the correct sequence of numbers in the gaps underneath. We have completed the first one for you.

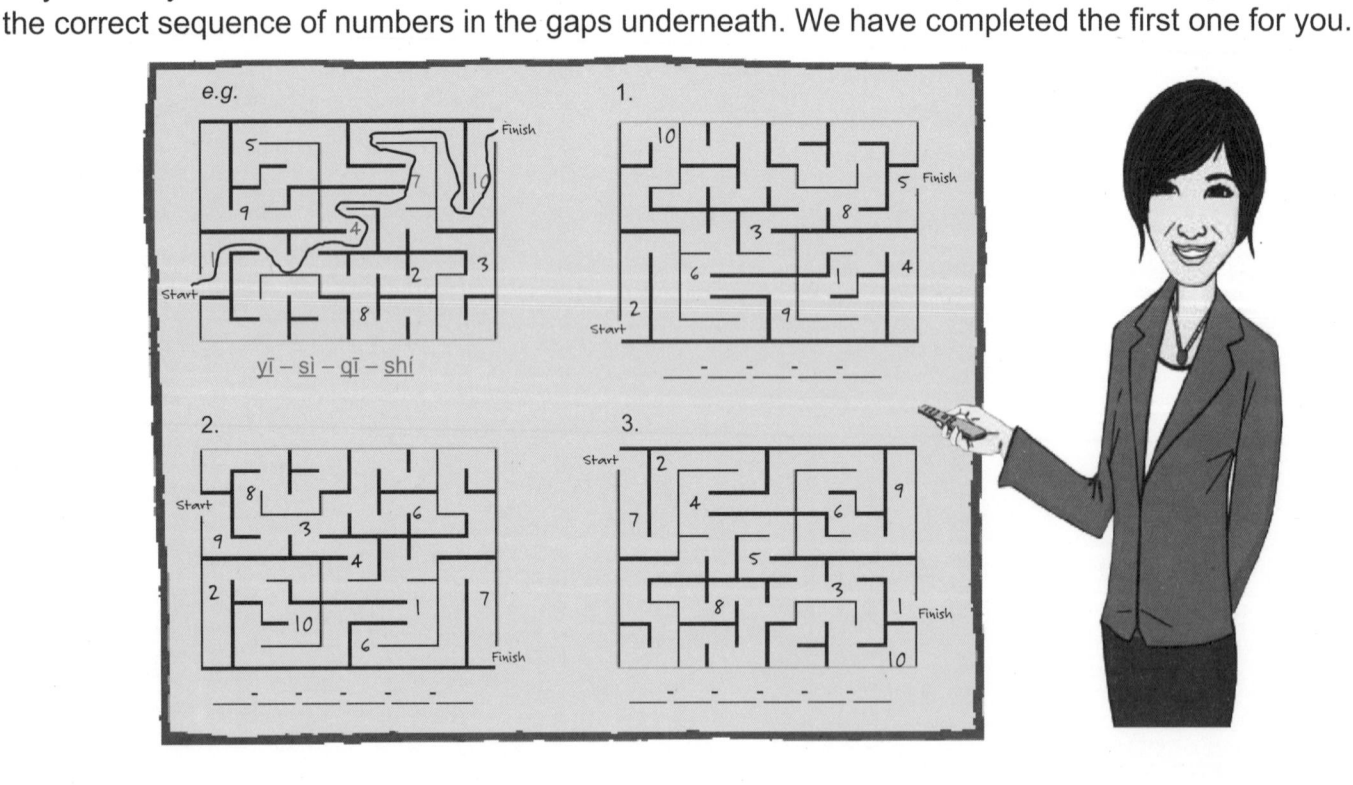

e.g. yī – sì – qī – shí

1. _ _ _ _ _ _

2. _ _ _ _ _ _

3. _ _ _ _ _ _

Exercise 2.3 - Katie's mobile number?
Katie has given her best friend, Xiǎo Jūn, her mobile number (see below). Help Katie write her mobile number in Chinese pinyin. We have completed zero for you.

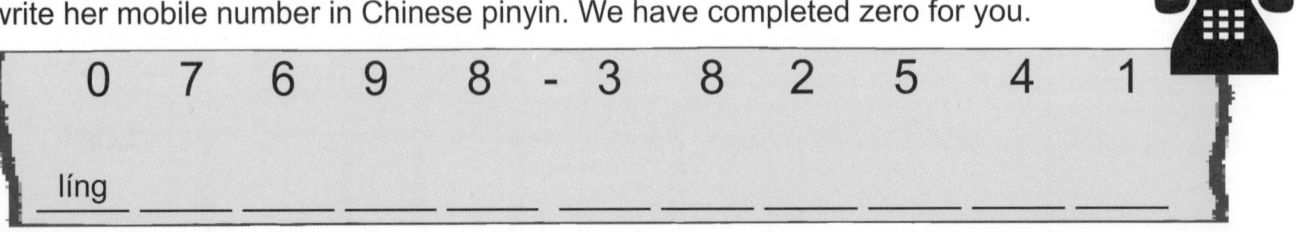

0 7 6 9 8 - 3 8 2 5 4 1

líng _ _ _ _ _ _ _ _ _ _ _

10 shí 十

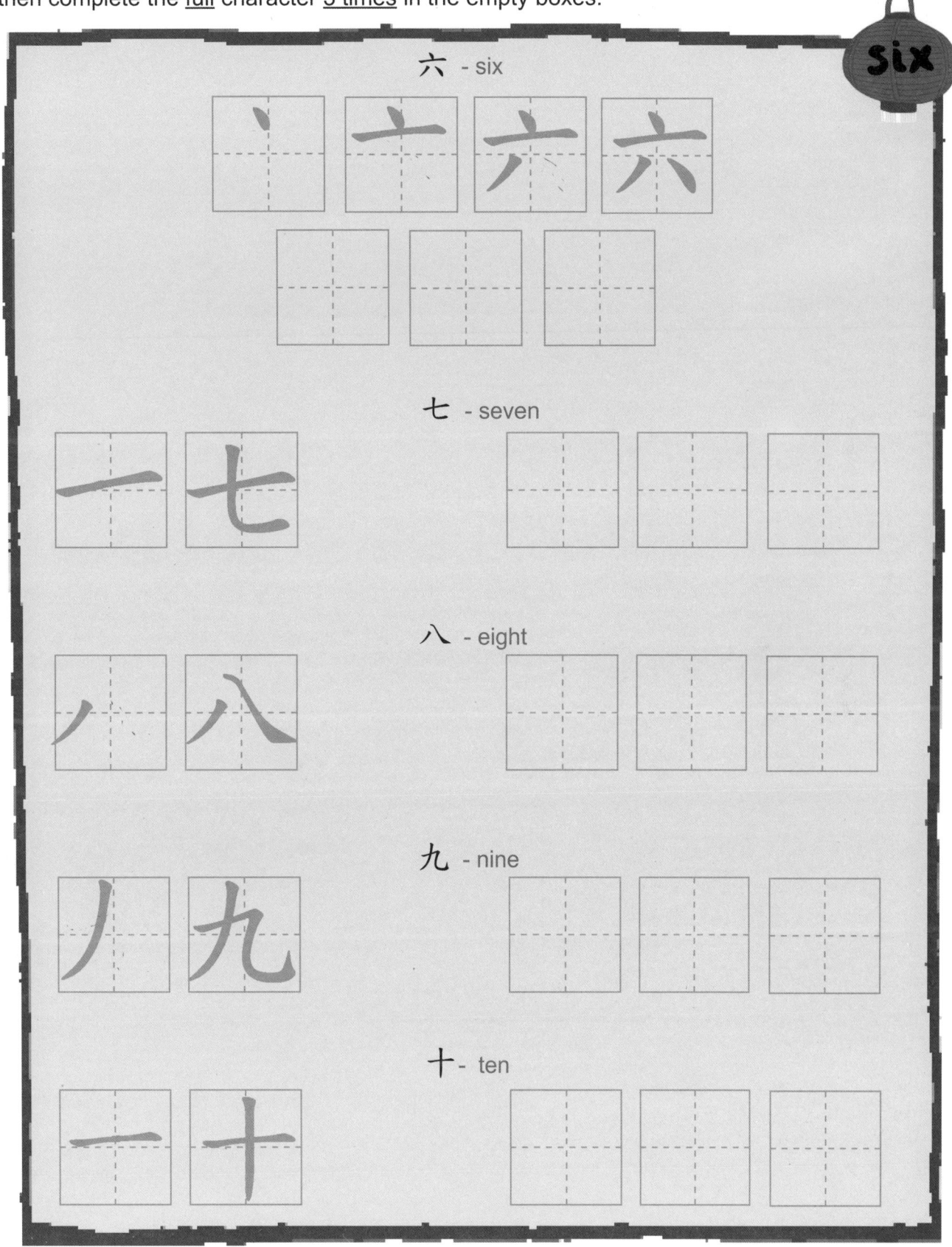

Unit 2

Writing the Chinese characters for 6-10

Exercise 2.4 – Writing 6-10 in Chinese characters
Practise writing the Chinese characters for numbers 6-10. First trace over the grey strokes and then complete the <u>full</u> character <u>3 times</u> in the empty boxes.

六 - six

七 - seven

八 - eight

九 - nine

十 - ten

11 *shíyī* 十一

Unit 2

Exercise 2.5 – Chinese numbers between 5 and 10
Fill in the boxes with the correct answers using Chinese characters. We have completed an example for you.

e.g. How many legs does an octopus have? 　　八

1. Snow White and the ___ dwarves?

2. Eighteen divided by three?

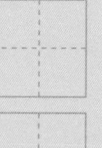

3. How many toes do you have in total?

4. What number do you ring three times for emergencies?

Numbers greater than 10 in Chinese

The numbers 11 to 99 are 'ten one' 'ten two' 'ten three' etc. in Chinese:

shíyī 十一 = 11	èrshí 二十 = 20	èrshí'èr 二十二 = 22
shí'èr 十二 = 12	sānshí 三十 = 30	sānshísān 三十三 = 33
shísān 十三... = 13	sìshí 四十... = 40	sìshísì 四十四... = 44

Exercise 2.6 – Chinese numbers greater than 10 using pinyin
Fill in the gaps with the correct answers in pinyin. We have completed an example for you.

e.g. the number of players in a football team?　　　shíyī

1. Number of months in a year?　　　_____

2. An unlucky number between 11 and 20?　　　_____

3. Christmas Day is on December __th?　　　_____

4. 9 x 9 - 23 = ?　　　_____

5. 6 x 5 x 3 = ?　　　_____

Exercise 2.7 – You will need your calculator!
Work out the answer for the maths question below and then complete the answer in pinyin in the spaces provided.

32 - 6 x 4 - 65 + 34 x 2 - 93 + 46

_____ _____ _____

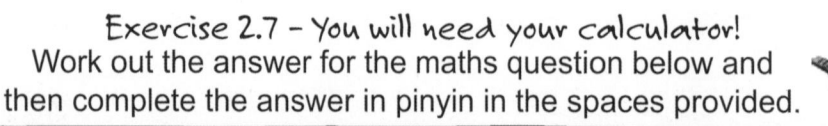

12 shí'èr 十二

Unit 2

Exercise 2.8 – What's missing?
Look below at the Chinese characters and complete the empty boxes. We have completed the first one for you.

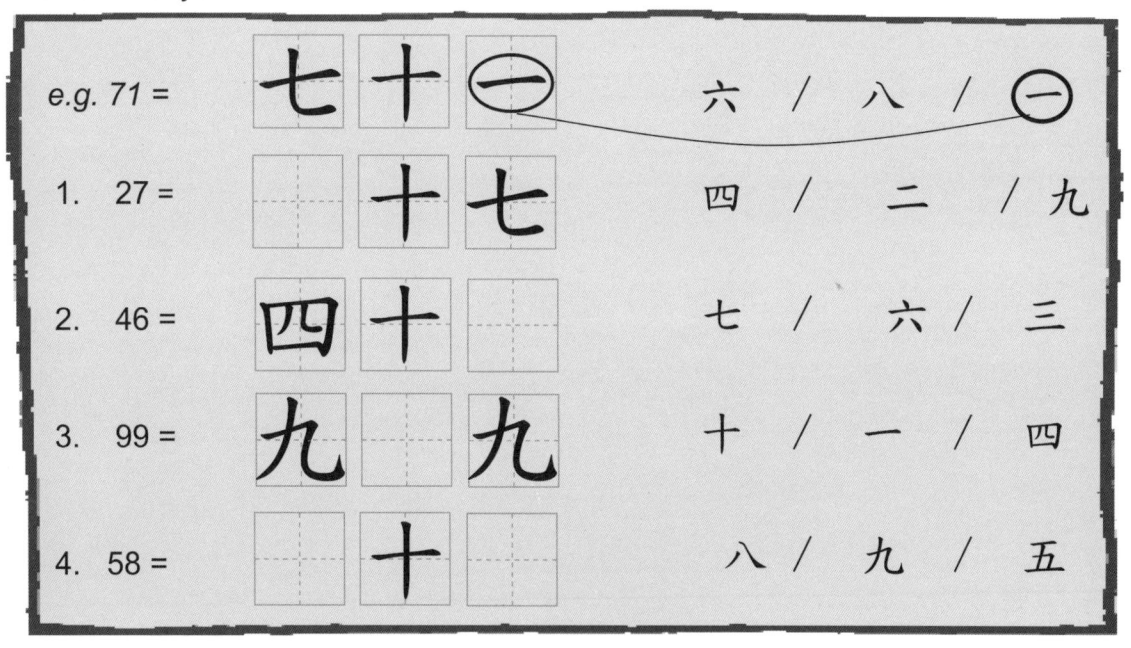

e.g. 71 =	七	十	一	六 / 八 / 一
1. 27 =		十	七	四 / 二 / 九
2. 46 =	四	十		七 / 六 / 三
3. 99 =	九		九	十 / 一 / 四
4. 58 =		十		八 / 九 / 五

How to say your name in Chinese

我	wǒ	=	I / me	什么	shénme?	= what?
你	nǐ	=	you	名字	míngzi	= name
他	tā	=	he	叫	jiào	= to be called (first name)
她	tā	=	she			

课本

Exercise 2.9 – Subject pronouns practice
Link the English words to the Chinese pinyin. Look at the words below and draw a line linking the correct Chinese and English pronouns. Make sure you also complete the English to Chinese section. Complete both exercises. We have completed the links between **tā** and 'he' for you!

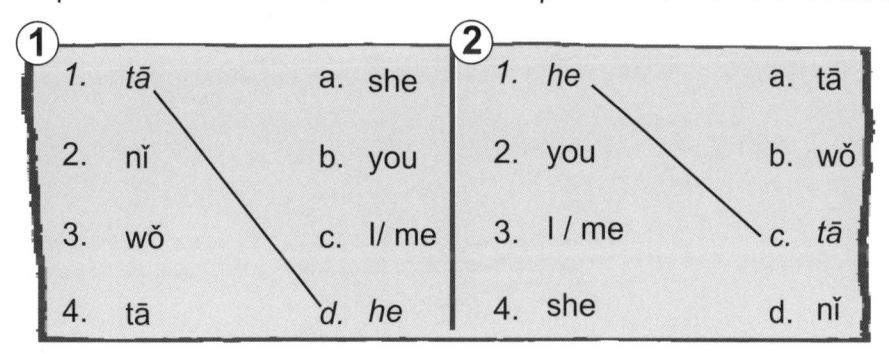

①
1. tā   a. she
2. nǐ   b. you
3. wǒ   c. I / me
4. tā   d. he

②
1. he   a. tā
2. you   b. wǒ
3. I / me   c. tā
4. she   d. nǐ

Exercise 2.10 – What's your name?
Look at the exercise below and complete the sentences with the missing Chinese words.
e.g. I am called Katie Reed = Wǒ jiào Katie Reed.

1. What is your name?	=	Nǐ jiào shénme _____?
2. What is your name?	=	Nǐ _____ _____ míngzi?
3. He is called Richard.	=	Tā _____ Richard.
4. What is her name?	=	_____ jiào shénme míngzi?
5. She is called Yángyang.	=	_____ _____ Yángyang.

13 shísān 十三

Unit 2

Exercise 2.11 – Let's practise writing 'I/me' and 'you' in Chinese characters
First trace over the grey strokes and then complete the full character <u>3 times</u> in the empty boxes.

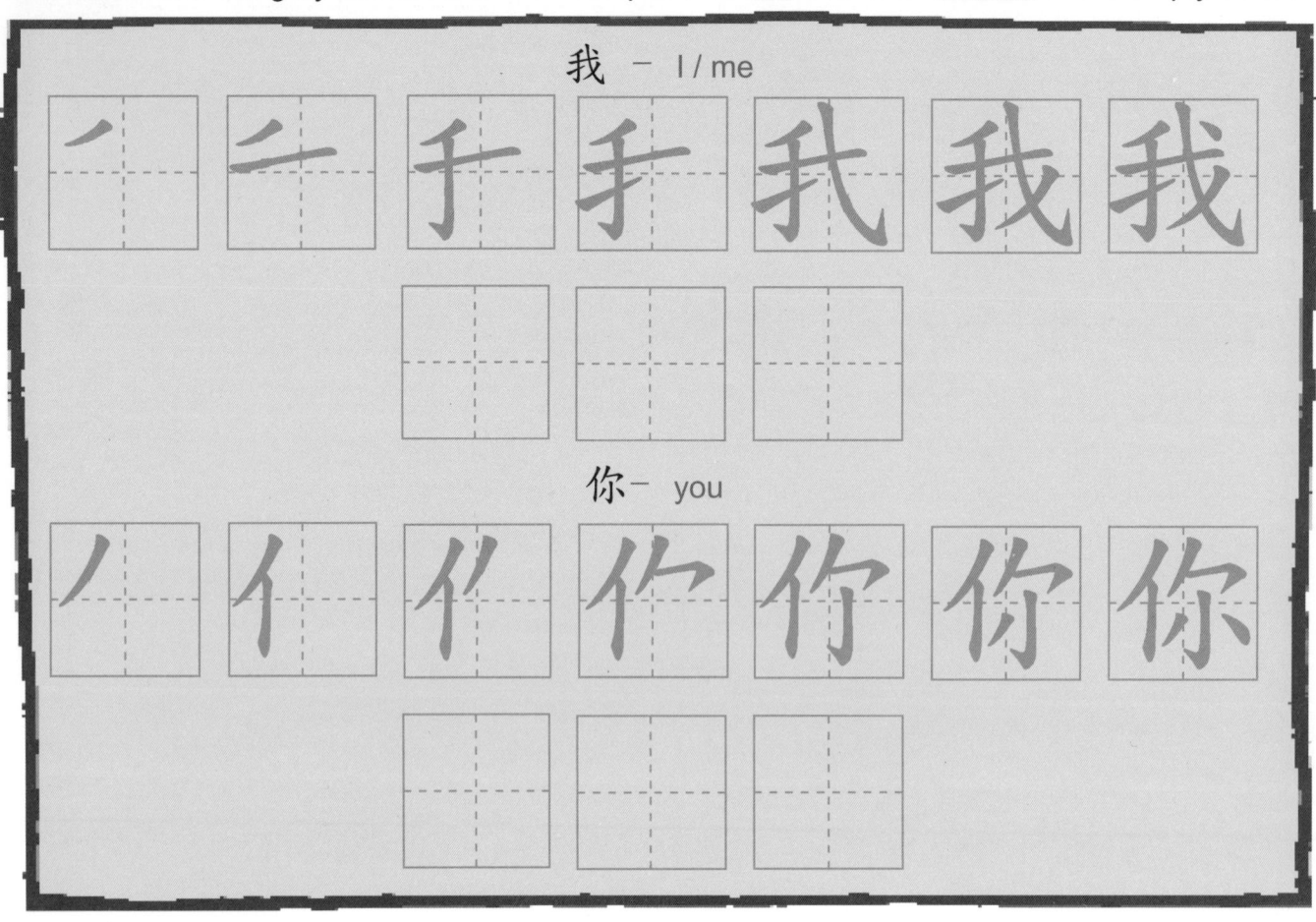

我 – I / me

你 – you

Exercise 2.12 – Fill in the boxes and blanks.
Using either the Chinese characters for <u>I/me</u> or <u>you</u>, complete all the boxes below. In addition, add the correct pinyin where necessary to complete the sentences. We have completed an example for you.

e.g. Hello   你 hǎo!

1. Hello   ☐ _____!

2. What is your name?   ☐ jiào shénme míngzi?

3. My name is William.   ☐ _____William.

4. What is your name?   ☐ _____?

5. My name is Katie.   ☐ _____ Katie.

14 shísì 十四

Unit 2

How to ask and say your age in Chinese

你几岁　Nǐ jǐ suì?　　= How old are you?

他几岁　Tā jǐ suì?　　= How old is he?

Structure: person + number + **suì**

我十二岁　Wǒ shí'èr suì.　　= I am 12 years old.

她十三岁　Tā shísān suì.　　= She is 13 years old.

你十九岁　Nǐ shíjiǔ suì.　　= You are 19 years old.

Exercise 2.13 – Saying how old you are in Chinese
Look at the English sentences on the left and link them to the correct Chinese sentences on the right. We have completed the first one for you.

1. I am 13 years old, he is 15 years old.
2. You are 52 years old, she is 35 years old.
3. She is 30 years old, I am 23 years old.
4. I am 74 years old, you are 19 years old.
5. He is 41 years old, she is 88 years old.

a. Tā sānshí suì, wǒ èrshísān suì.
b. Wǒ qīshísì suì, nǐ shíjiǔ suì.
c. Tā sìshíyī suì, tā bāshíbā suì.
d. Wǒ shísān suì, tā shíwǔ suì.
e. Nǐ wǔshí'èr suì, tā sānshíwǔ suì.

Exercise 2.14 – More 'age' practice - fill in the blanks
Work out how old everyone is in the sentences below. Write the answer in pinyin. We have completed an example for you.

Richard = 42　　Yúnyun = 45　　Shū = 44　　William = 16　　Guóyīng = 15

e.g. Mǎlì is 7 years younger than Guóyīng. How old is Mǎlì?　Tā __bā__ suì.

1. Mǐn is 5 years younger than William. How old is Mǐn?　Tā _____ _____ suì.

2. Jack is 2 years younger than William. How old is Jack?　Tā _____ suì.

3. Sandra is 5 years younger than Shū. How old is Shū?　Tā _____ _____ _____ suì.

4. Zhīlín is 6 years older than Yúnyun. How old is Zhīlín?　Tā _____ _____ suì.

Exercise 2.15 – Let's practise writing 'suì' in Chinese characters
First trace over the grey strokes and then complete the full character 3 times in the empty boxes.

岁 = age

15 shíwǔ 十五

Unit 2

Exercise 2.16 – How old are you?
Using pinyin and Chinese characters, write your age in the spaces and boxes below. Remember the structure '**Wǒ** + number + **suì**'.

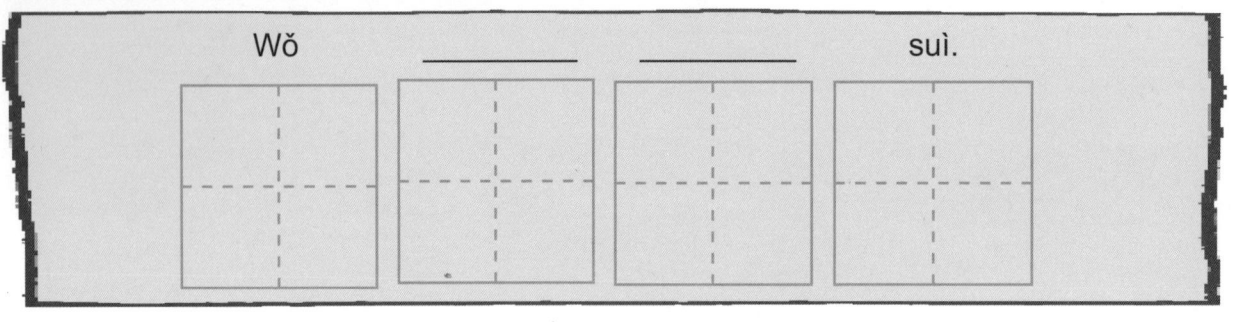

Wǒ _____ _____ suì.

Exercise 2.17 – Saying how old you are (using Chinese characters)
Look at the ages and then work out how old everyone is in the sentences below. Write the answers using Chinese characters. We have completed an example for you.

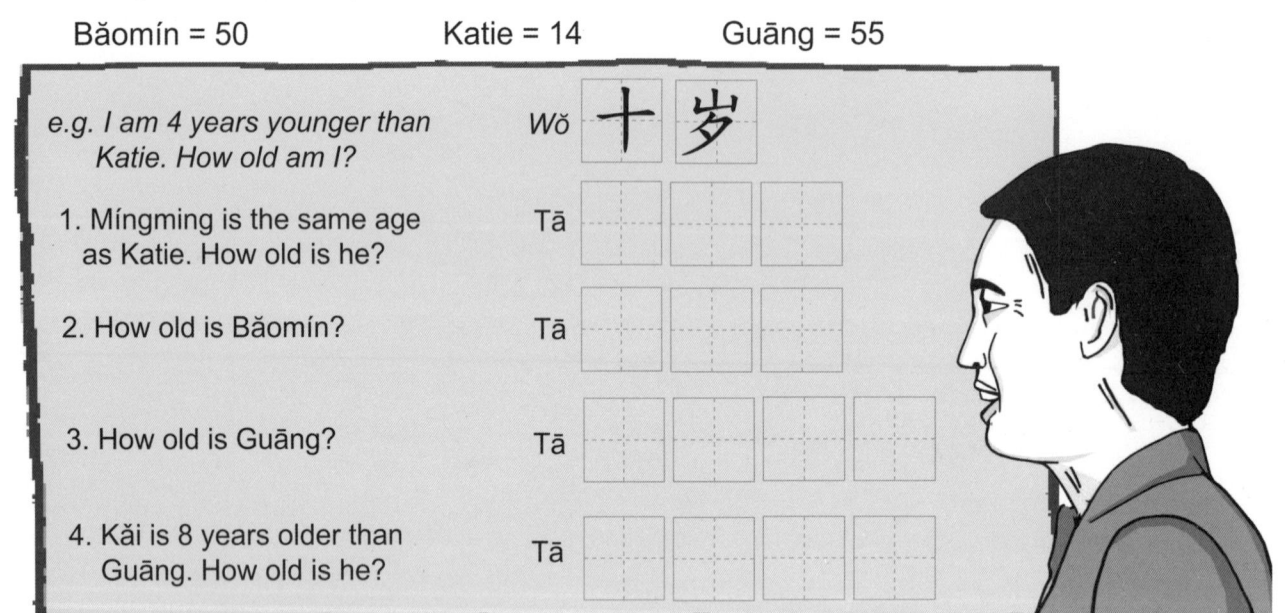

Bǎomín = 50   Katie = 14   Guāng = 55

e.g. I am 4 years younger than Katie. How old am I?   Wǒ 十 岁

1. Míngming is the same age as Katie. How old is he?   Tā

2. How old is Bǎomín?   Tā

3. How old is Guāng?   Tā

4. Kǎi is 8 years older than Guāng. How old is he?   Tā

Exercise 2.18 – Reading comprehension – different people's ages
Read through the passage and then answer the questions to the right in English. We have completed an example for you.

我 叫 Richard – 我 四十二 岁。她 叫 阳 阳 – 她
Wǒ jiào   wǒ shí   suì Tā jiào Yáng yang tā

三十八 岁。我 叫 之林 – 我 五十一 岁。她 叫 云云
shí bā suì   Wǒ jiào Zhī lín. wǒ shí   suì   Tā jiào Yún yun

– 她 四十五 岁。
  tā shí   suì

e.g. How old is Richard?   42

1. Which of the 4 people is 45 years old? _____

2. How much older is Zhīlín than Richard? _____

3. Who is the youngest person of the four? _____

4. Who is the oldest person of the four? _____

16 shíliù 十六

Unit 2

The origins of 人 in Chinese

The word for 'person' or **rén** in Chinese looks like a stick-man with no arms. Here is a quick reminder of the evolution.

课本

Exercise 2.19 – Let's practise writing 'person' in Chinese characters
First trace over the grey strokes and then complete the full character 3 times in the empty boxes.

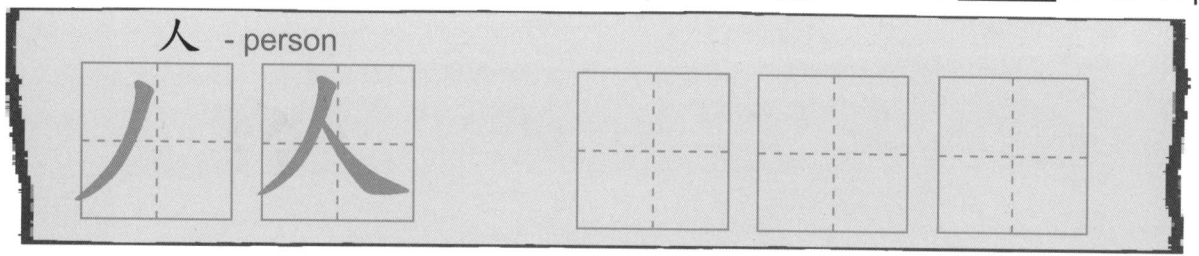

人 - person

Exercise 2.20 – How many people?
Below you will find 2 images with the Chinese character 人 written multiple times. First count the number of 人 in each image and then write down the answer in Chinese characters below.

Number of 人:

Number of 人:

The four different Chinese 'e' tones

'E' is pronounced very differently in Chinese to English, like 'err' but with your tongue right down. Here are some examples of 'e' words that use the 1st, 2nd, 3rd and 4th tones.

1st tone example:	chē	=	car
2nd tone example:	shé	=	snake
3rd tone example:	kě	=	thirsty
4th tone example:	rè	=	hot

课本

Exercise 2.21 – Recognising the 4 different 'e' tones
Look at the grids below and circle all the words with the correct tone. We have completed an example for you.

e.g. hot

(rè)	rě	ré
(rè)	ré	rě
rē	(rè)	(rè)
rě	rě	(rè)
ré	(rè)	ré

1. thirsty

kē	ké	kě
kē	kè	kě
ké	kē	kě
ké	ké	kè
kě	kē	ké

2. car

chē	chē	chē
chē	chè	chē
ché	chē	chē
chē	chè	chē
ché	chē	ché

3. snake

shé	shé	Shé
shē	shè	shě
shé	shé	shè
shē	shē	shé
shé	shè	shě

17 shíqī 十七

Unit 2

How to say 'also' in Chinese - yě

我很好。 她也很好。
Wǒ hěn hǎo. Tā yě hěn hǎo. = I am well. She is also well.

他叫小军。 他也叫小军。
Tā jiào Xiǎojūn. Tā yě jiào Xiǎojūn. = He is called Xiǎojūn. He is also called Xiǎojūn.

我十六岁。 我也十六岁。
Wǒ shíliù suì. Wǒ yě shíliù suì. = I am 16 years old. He is also 16 years old.

Exercise 2.22 – Using yě

For each statement below you must circle the sentence that would most likely follow. We have completed an example for you.

e.g. Wǒ shí'èr suì. (I am twelve years old.)
a) Wǒ yě shí'èr suì.
b) Wǒ yě shí suì.
c) **Nǐ yě shíyī suì.** (circled)

1. Wǒ hěn hǎo.
   a) Nǐ hǎo ma?
   b) Wǒ yě hěn hǎo.
   c) Nǐ jiào shénme?

2. Tā jiào Richard.
   a) Wǒ jiào Richard.
   b) Nǐ yě jiào Richard ma?
   c) Wǒ yě jiào Richard.

3. Wǒ jiǔ suì.
   a) Nǐ ne?
   b) Nǐ yě shí suì.
   c) Nǐ yě jiǔ suì.

Exercise 2.23 - Putting the sentences in the right order

Below you will see parts of a typical Chinese conversation between two people meeting for the first time. They are out of sequence - put them in the correct order by writing numbers 1-6 in the spaces on the right. We have completed the first one for you.

Wǒ yě shísì suì	___
Wǒ jiào Míngming, nǐ ne?	___
Wǒ jiào Katie, nǐ jǐ suì?	___
Wǒ shísì suì. Nǐ ne?	___
Nǐ hǎo	1
Nǐ hǎo, nǐ jiào shénme míngzi?	___

Exercise 2.24 – Let's practise writing 'also' in Chinese characters

First trace over the grey strokes and then complete the full character 3 times in the empty boxes.

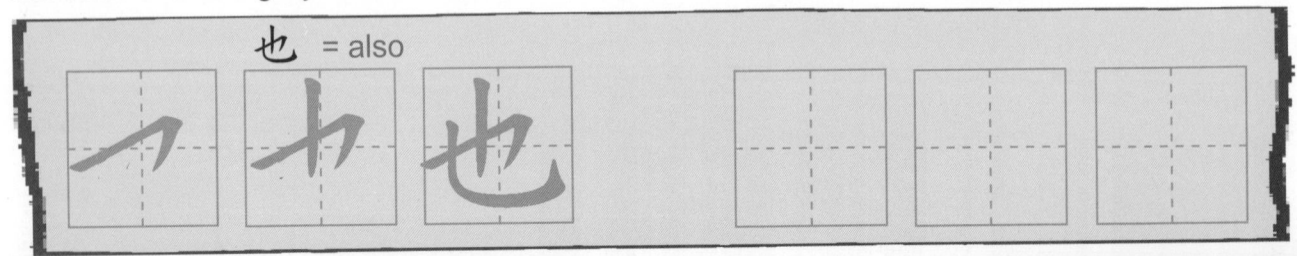

也 = also

18 shíbā 十八

Unit 2

Exercise 2.25 – I am also 10 years old
Below are 4 short dialogues of people who are both the same age. Using Chinese characters write the correct sentence incorporating 我 也 + age + 岁 in the blank boxes. We have completed an example for you.

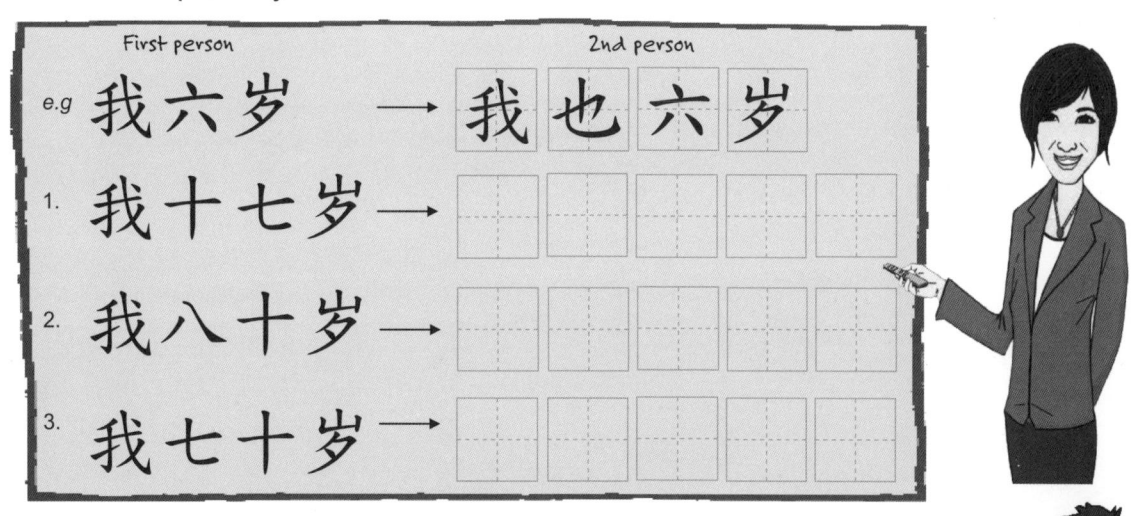

First person / 2nd person

e.g. 我六岁 → 我也六岁
1. 我十七岁 →
2. 我八十岁 →
3. 我七十岁 →

Saying 'friend' in Chinese

朋友	péngyou	= friend
我朋友	wǒ péngyou	= my friend
你朋友	nǐ péngyou	= your friend
他朋友	tā péngyou	= his friend
她朋友	tā péngyou	= her friend

课本

Exercise 2.26 – She is my friend!
Below you will find some sentences in English on the left. Translate the sentences into Chinese and write the answers in the gaps on the right. We have completed an example for you.

e.g.	My friend is called Mǐn.	Wǒ ___péngyou___ ___jiào___ Mǐn.
1.	Your friend is called Richard.	Nǐ _____ _____ Richard.
2.	Her friend is called Yángyang.	_____ _____ jiào _____.
3.	His friend is called William.	_____ _____ _____ William.
4.	My friend is called Guóyīng.	_____ _____ _____ _____.

Exercise 2.27 – Let's practise writing 'friend' in Chinese characters
First trace over the grey strokes and then complete the full character 3 times in the empty boxes.

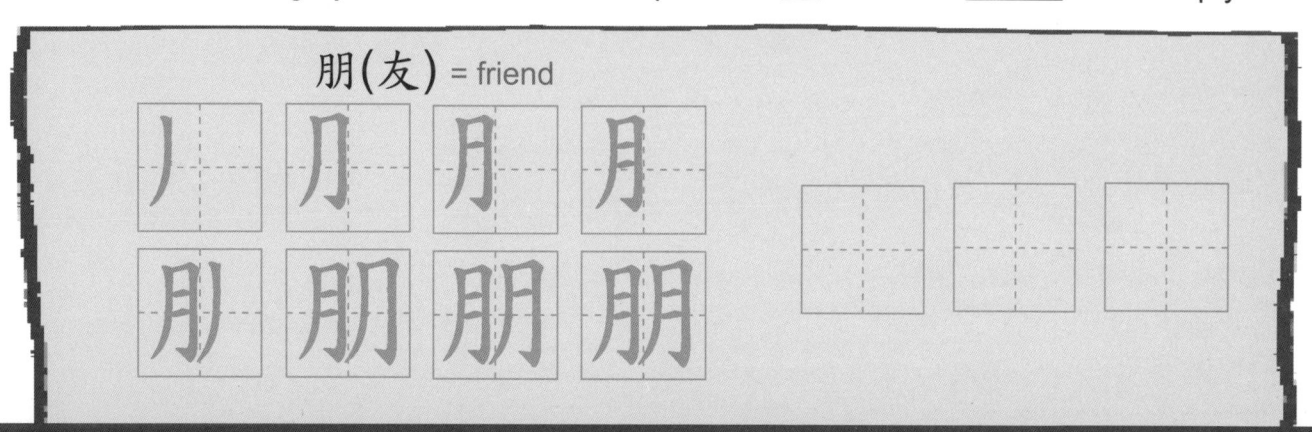

朋(友) = friend

丿 月 月 月
月 朋 朋 朋

19 shíjiǔ 十九

Unit 2

(朋)友 = friend

一 ナ 方 友

Exercise 2.28 – Writing 'my friend' in Chinese characters

Below you find some short sentences in English. Using a mixture of Chinese characters and pinyin, please complete the empty boxes and spaces below. We have completed an example for you.

e.g. Your friend is called Xiǎoyù.   你 朋 友   ___jiào___ Xiǎoyù.

1. My friend is called Mǐn.   _____ Mǐn.

2. Your friend is called Dà Wěi.   _____ Dà Wěi.

3. My friend is called Katie.   _____ Katie.

Famous Tourist Attractions in China

Exercise 2.29 – Famous tourist attractions in China

What do you remember from Unit 2? Rely on your memory or use the internet to choose the correct answers below! We have completed an example for you.

e.g. What is the name of the Great Wall of China in Mandarin Chinese?

a) Chéng Chéng ☐
b) Cháng Cháng ☐
c) Cháng Chéng ☑

1. Why did the Chinese build the Great Wall of China?

a) to make China the most powerful nation on the planet ☐
b) to make China more beautiful ☐
c) to protect themselves from raids from Northern Tribes ☐

2. When did the Chinese first start building the Great Wall of China?

a) during the Han dynasty ☐
b) end of the Ming dynasty ☐
c) 19th century ☐

20 èrshí 二十

3. What is the Terracotta Army?

a) the name of China's national armed guard
b) the name of a well containing life-size clay statues of warriors
c) the name of the Chinese President's bodyguards.

4. What does Xī'ān mean?

a) Western peace
b) The temple of peace
c) The peaceful Buddha

5. Northern China….

a) is the hottest part of China
b) is not as mild as Southern China
c) has more mountains and scenery than Southern China

Unit 2

21 èrshíyī 二十一

Unit 3

UNIT 3 - MY FAMILY

Exercise 3.1 - Do you remember?
Look at the words below and find the translations for the family and family members.
We have completed 'home/family' for you.

1. home/family
2. dad
3. mum
4. older brother
5. older sister
6. younger brother
7. younger sister

a. 妹妹 mèimei
b. 弟弟 dìdi
c. 妈妈 māma
d. 哥哥 jiějie
e. 姐姐 gēge
f. 爸爸 bàba
g. 家 jiā

Exercise 3.2 - Family Crossword
Fill in the Chinese pinyin in the crossword below search using the key on the right hand side.
Don't forget to add the tones. We have completed 1-down for you.

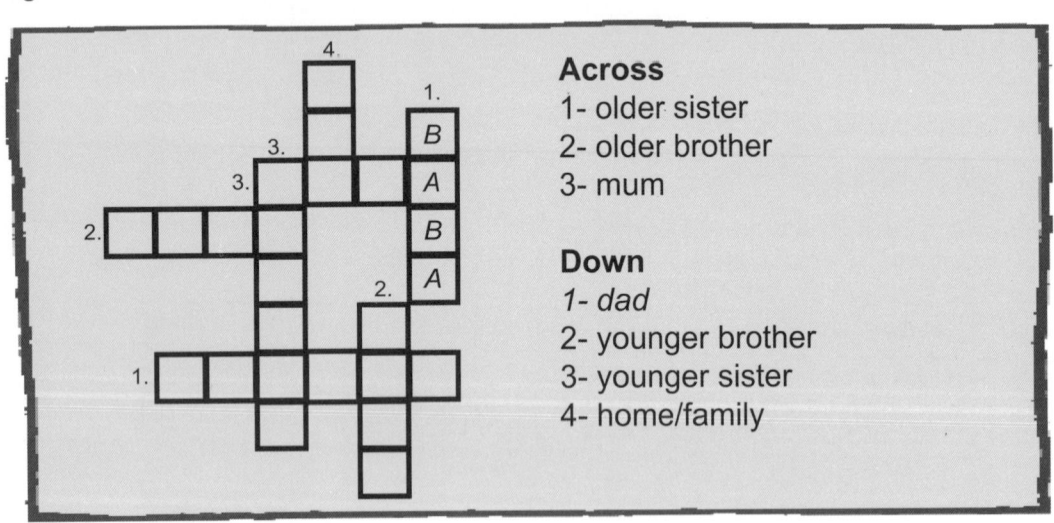

Across
1- older sister
2- older brother
3- mum

Down
1- dad
2- younger brother
3- younger sister
4- home/family

Exercise 3.3 - Family Search
Try to spot all the above family members in pinyin in the wordsearch below. Don't forget to add the tones. We have located the word for 'home/family' for you.

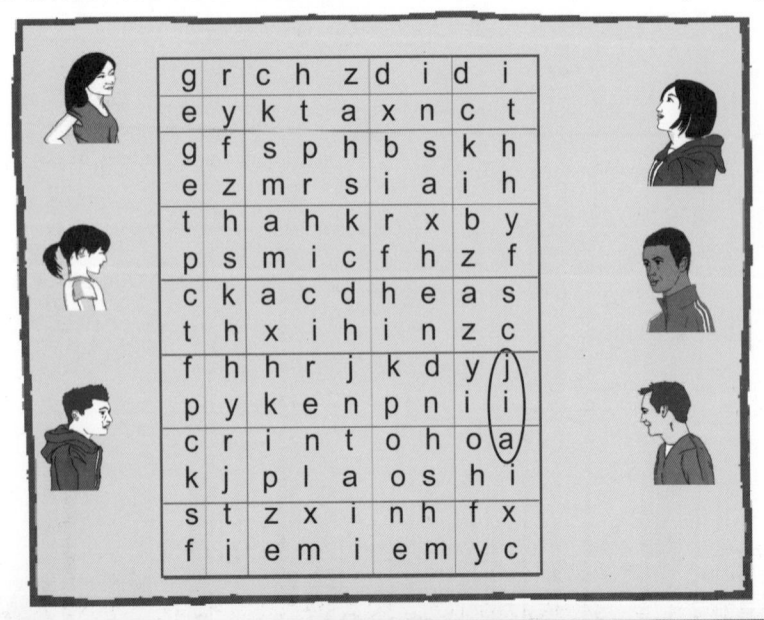

g	r	c	h	z	d	i	d	i
e	y	k	t	a	x	n	c	t
g	f	s	p	h	b	s	k	h
e	z	m	r	s	i	a	i	h
t	h	a	h	k	r	x	b	y
p	s	m	i	c	f	h	z	f
c	k	a	c	d	h	e	a	s
t	h	x	i	h	i	n	z	c
f	h	h	r	j	k	d	y	j
p	y	k	e	n	p	n	i	i
c	r	i	n	t	o	h	o	a
k	j	p	l	a	o	s	h	i
s	t	z	x	i	n	h	f	x
f	i	e	m	i	e	m	y	c

Can you find the mystery word? Clue: you'll need one to teach you Chinese!

_____

Translate the word into **English** that appears twice:

_____

22 èrshí'èr 二十二

Unit 3

Family and Age

Exercise 3.4 – Xiǎoyù's family
Complete the sentences on the right according to the names of Xiǎoyù's family members. We have completed an example for you.

e.g. Hello, how are you?.	Nǐ hǎo nǐ hǎo ma?
1. I am called Xiǎoyù.	_____ jiào _____.
2. Mum is called Yúnyun.	_____ jiào Yúnyun.
3. Older brother is called Xiǎojūn.	_____ _____ Xiǎojūn.
4. Dad is called Bǎomín.	_____ _____ _____.

Exercise 3.5 – Let's meet Katie and Xiǎoyù's parents!
Look at the details for both Katie and Xiǎoyù's families and then indicate if the following sentences are true or false. We have completed an example for you.

Katie's parents:

Bàba jiào Richard. (sìshí'èr suì)
Māma jiào Sandra. (sānshíjiǔ suì)

Xiǎoyù's parents:

Bàba jiào Bǎomín. (wǔshí suì)
Māma jiào Yúnyun. (sìshíwǔ suì)

e.g. Xiǎoyù's dad is younger than Katie's dad.	True ☐	False ☑
1. Katie's dad is called Richard and Xiǎoyù's father is called Bǎomín.	True ☐	False ☐
2. Xiǎoyù's mum is called Sandra?	True ☐	False ☐
3. Katie's mum is only 1 year younger than Xiǎoyù's mum.	True ☐	False ☐
4. Xiǎoyù's dad is 8 years older than Richard.	True ☐	False ☐

My, yours, his, hers

我妈妈	wǒ māma	=	my mother
你姐姐	nǐ jiějie	=	your older sister
他爸爸	tā bàba	=	his dad
她弟弟	tā dìdi	=	her younger brother

课本

Exercise 3.6 – Select the correct answer
Match the English on the left with one of the pinyin on the right. Circle the correct answer. We have completed an example for you.

e.g. her little sister	tā māma	(tā mèimei)	tā jiějie	tā gēge
1. his Dad	wǒ bàba	tā jiějie	tā bàba	tā māma
2. my big brother	nǐ gēge	wǒ bàba	tā jiějie	wǒ gēge
3. your little brother	tā dìdi	nǐ dìdi	wǒ jiějie	wǒ bàba
4. her Mum	wǒ māma	tā gēge	tā bàba	tā māma

23 èrshísān 二十三

Unit 3

Exercise 3.7 – Let's practise writing 'mum' and 'dad' in Chinese characters
First trace over the grey strokes and then complete the <u>full</u> characters <u>3 times</u> in the empty boxes.

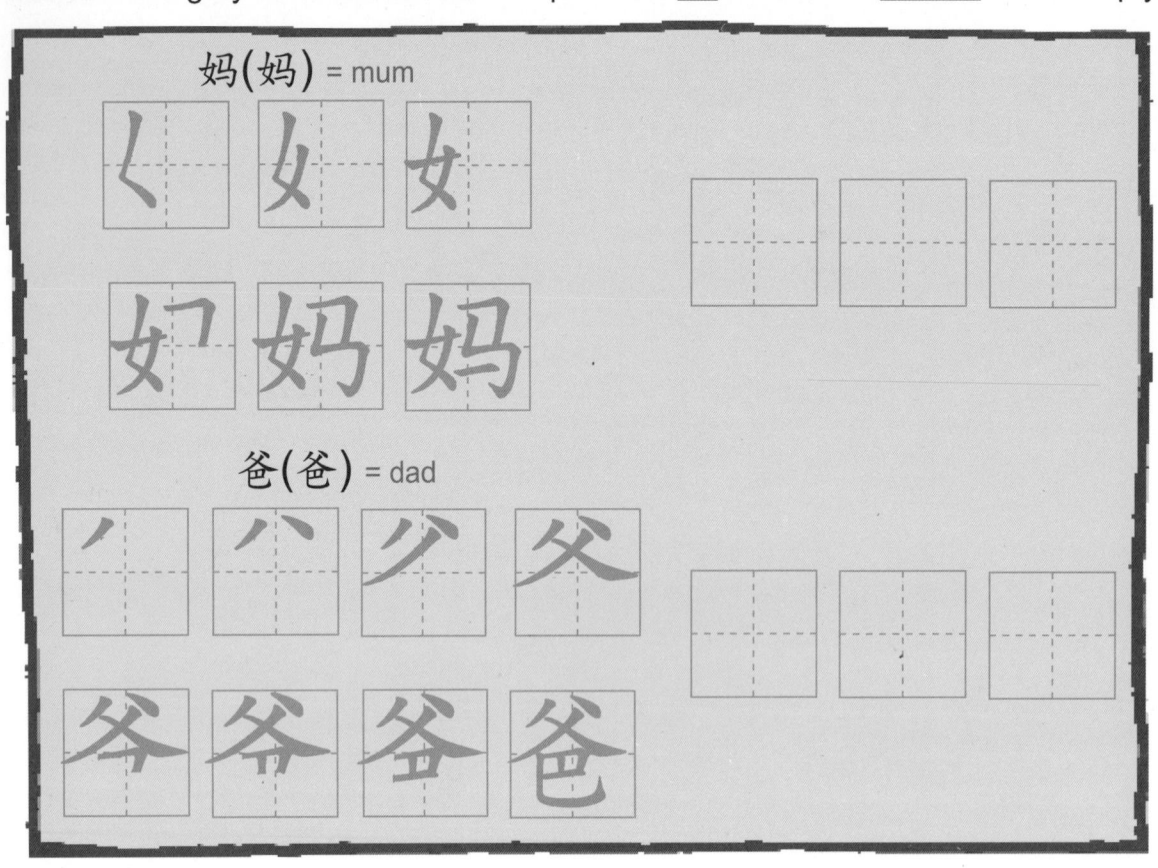

妈(妈) = mum

爸(爸) = dad

Exercise 3.8 – Practise writing 妈妈 and 爸爸 with age
Read the short English sentences and translate them into Chinese characters. We have completed an example for you.

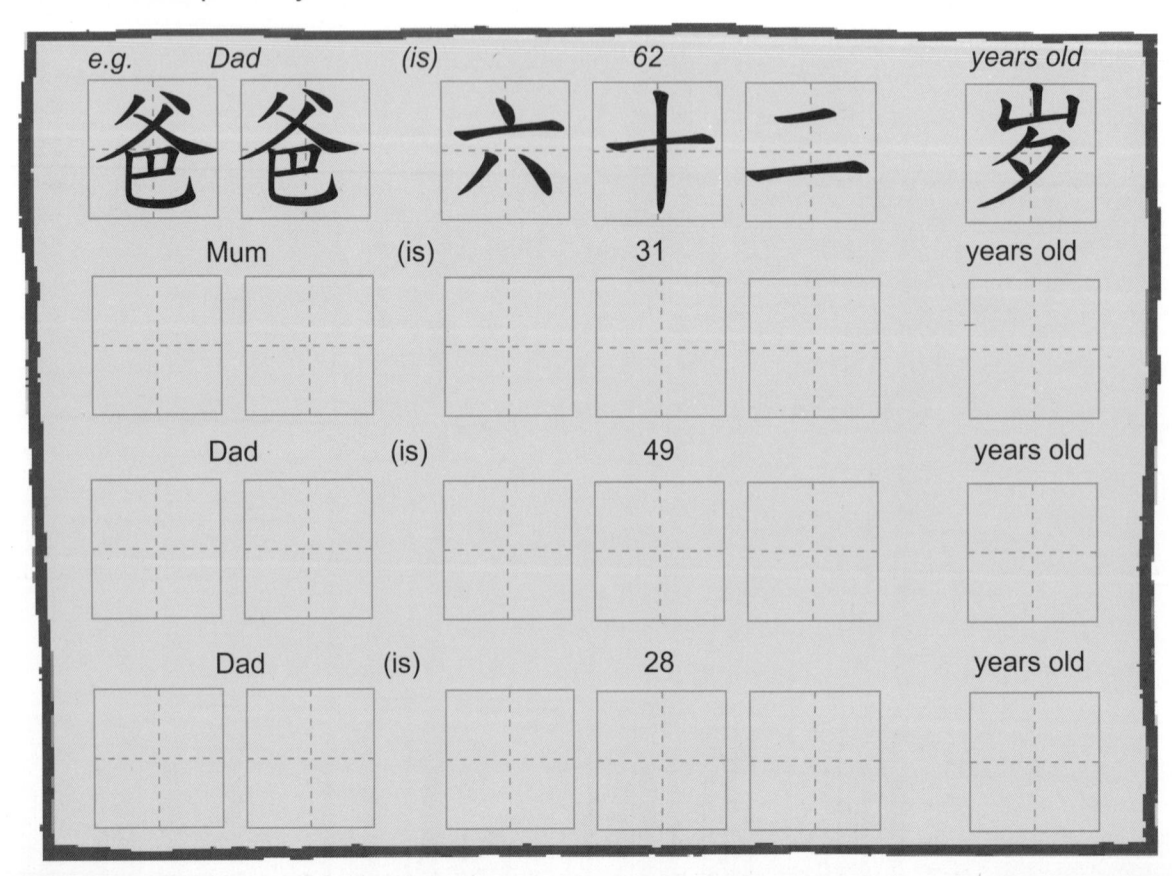

e.g. Dad (is) 62 years old

爸 爸 六 十 二 岁

Mum (is) 31 years old

Dad (is) 49 years old

Dad (is) 28 years old

24 èrshísì 二十四

Unit 3

Saying 'have' and 'don't have' in Chinese

我有弟弟	Wǒ yǒu dìdi.	=	I have a younger brother.
你没有哥哥	Nǐ méiyǒu gēge.	=	You don't have an older brother.
他有姐姐	Tā yǒu jiějie.	=	He has an older sister.
她没有妹妹	Tā méiyǒu mèimei.	=	She doesn't have a younger sister.

课本

Exercise 3.9 – Practise saying yǒu and méiyǒu

For each item below state whether or not you have one of the listed items by circling either **yǒu** or **méiyǒu**. We have completed the first one for you.

e.g. watch	yǒu	méiyǒu
1) dog	**(yǒu)**	méiyǒu
2) mobile phone	yǒu	méiyǒu
3) cat	yǒu	méiyǒu
4) plane	yǒu	méiyǒu
5) television	yǒu	méiyǒu
6) monkey	yǒu	méiyǒu

Exercise 3.10 – Practise saying yǒu and méiyǒu

Create the correct link between the Chinese pinyin on the left and the English sentences on the right. We have completed the first one for you.

1. Wǒ yǒu dìdi.
2. Māma méiyǒu mèimei.
3. Dìdi méiyǒu jiějie.
4. Tā yǒu gēge.
5. Bàba yǒu dìdi.
6. Nǐ méiyǒu jiějie.

a. He has an older brother.
b. You don't have an older sister.
c. I have a younger brother.
d. Younger brother does not have an older sister.
e. Mum does not have a younger sister.
f. Dad has a younger brother.

Exercise 3.11 – Write 'have' and 'not have' in Chinese characters

First trace over the grey strokes and then complete the <u>full</u> characters <u>3 times</u> in the empty boxes.

有 = to have

没(有) = to not have

25 èrshíwǔ 二十五

Unit 3

Exercise 3.12 - 有 or 没有?
Look at the short statements below and write either 有 or 没有 to give the sentences the correct meaning. We have completed an example for you.

e.g. An elephant —— 有 —— a trunk.

1. An hour —— —— 62 minutes.
2. Sharks —— —— fins.
3. Cars —— —— 5 wheels.
4. A school —— —— teachers

Asking questions using ma

| 你有姐姐吗？ | Nǐ yǒu jiějie ma? | = | Do you have an older sister? |
| 我没有姐姐， 我有妹妹 | Wǒ méiyǒu jiějie, Wǒ yǒu mèimei. | = | I do not have an older sister, I have a younger sister. |

Exercise 3.13 - Choose the correct answer
For each of the questions below, you must circle which of the two answers <u>makes sense</u>. Please watch out for the negatives and the positives! We have completed an example for you.

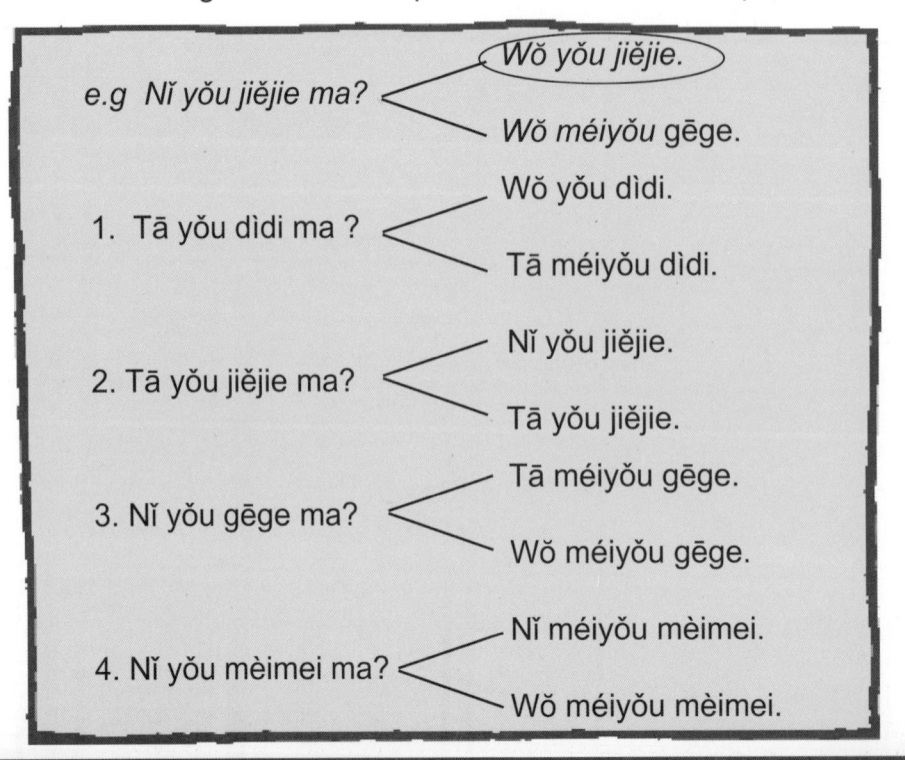

e.g Nǐ yǒu jiějie ma?
- (Wǒ yǒu jiějie.)
- Wǒ méiyǒu gēge.

1. Tā yǒu dìdi ma?
- Wǒ yǒu dìdi.
- Tā méiyǒu dìdi.

2. Tā yǒu jiějie ma?
- Nǐ yǒu jiějie.
- Tā yǒu jiějie.

3. Nǐ yǒu gēge ma?
- Tā méiyǒu gēge.
- Wǒ méiyǒu gēge.

4. Nǐ yǒu mèimei ma?
- Nǐ méiyǒu mèimei.
- Wǒ méiyǒu mèimei.

26 èrshíliù 二十六

Unit 3

Exercise 3.14 - Write the question particle 'ma' in Chinese characters.
First trace over the grey strokes and then complete the <u>full</u> characters <u>3 times</u> in the empty boxes.

吗 = question particle 'ma'

Exercise 3.15 - Do you have sisters? Link the English to the characters
Match up the English questions on the left to the Chinese character translations on the right.
Note: older sister = 姐姐；younger sister = 妹妹. We have completed the first one for you.

1. Does Dad have a younger sister?   a. 你有妹妹吗？
2. Does Mum have an older sister?   b. 爸爸有姐姐吗？
3. Do you have an older sister?   c. 爸爸有妹妹吗？
4. Does Dad have an older sister?   d. 妈妈有妹妹吗？
5. Does Mum have a younger sister?   e. 你有姐姐吗？
6. Do you have a younger sister?   f. 妈妈有姐姐吗？

Exercise 3.16 - Practise using 吗 when asking about age
Translate each of the English sentences using Chinese characters – don't forget to use 吗!
We have completed an example for you.

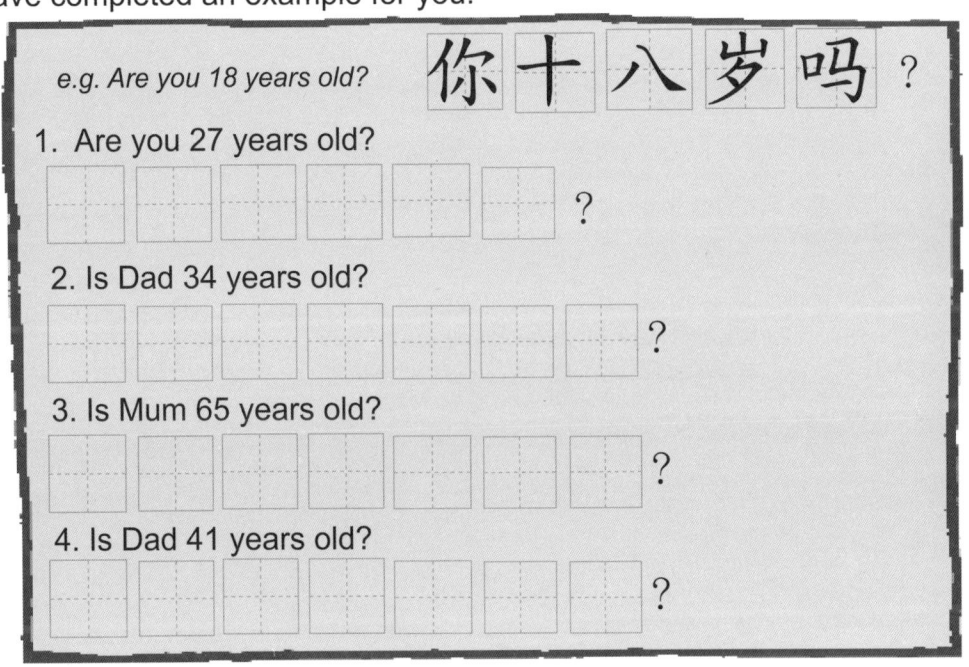

e.g. Are you 18 years old?   你 十 八 岁 吗 ?

1. Are you 27 years old?
2. Is Dad 34 years old?
3. Is Mum 65 years old?
4. Is Dad 41 years old?

Exercise 3.17 - Write 'home/family' in Chinese characters
First trace over the grey strokes and then complete the <u>full</u> character <u>3 times</u> in the empty boxes.

家 = home/family

27 èrshíqī 二十七

Unit 3

Exercise 3.18 - Missing strokes
You have just written the Chinese character for 'home/family' - 家. Look at the six incomplete versions of this character and circle the area where a stroke is missing. We have completed the first one for you.

Exercise 3.19 - Write 'he' and 'she' in Chinese characters
First trace over the grey strokes and then complete the <u>full</u> characters <u>3 times</u> in the empty boxes.

他 = he

她 = she

Exercise 3.20 - Practise writing 他 and 她
For each of the sentences below you must translate the English sentence into Chinese using the corresponding Chinese characters and pinyin where necessary. We have completed an example for you.

	She	is called	Katie.	Her	mum	is called	Sandra.
e.g.	她	_jiào_	Katie.	她 妈 妈		_jiào_	Sandra.

	He	is called	Mǐn.	His	dad	is called	Guāng.
1.		____	Mǐn.			____	Guāng.

	She	is called	Jìng.	She	(is)	17 years old
2.		____	Jìng.			

	He	is called	Zhīlín.	He	(is)	51 years old
3.		____	Zhīlín.			

Unit 3

Exercise 3.21 – Reading comprehension: How old are they?
Read through the passage and answer the questions in <u>English</u>. We have completed an example for you.

我 叫 小玉。我 十 岁。
　　 jiào Xiǎo yù

我 爸爸 叫 保民。他 五十 岁。
　 bà ba　jiào　Bǎo mín　Tā

我 妈妈 叫 云云。她 四十五 岁。
　 mā ma　jiào　Yún yun　Tā

我 哥哥 叫 小军。他 十六 岁。
　 gē ge　jiào　Xiǎo jūn　Tā

我 没有 弟弟，我 没有 妹妹。
　 méi yǒu dì di　　méi yǒu mèi mei

e.g. How old is Xiǎoyù? _____10 years old_____

1. How old is Xiǎoyù's dad? _____

2. How old is Xiǎoyù's mum? _____

3. How old is Xiǎoyù's older brother? _____

4. How old is Xiǎoyù's younger sister? _____

Exercise 3.22 – Reading comprehension: Guóyīng's family
Read through the passage and answer the questions in <u>English</u>. We have completed an example for you.

我 叫 国英。我 十五 岁。
　 jiào Guó yīng

我 有 爸爸。他 叫 之林。他 五十一 岁。
　 yǒu　bà ba　Tā　jiào　Zhī lín　Tā

我 有 妈妈。她 叫 晨晨。她 五十 岁。
　 yǒu mā ma　Tā　jiào Chén chen　Tā

我 有 妹妹。她 叫 马丽。她 八 岁。
　 yǒu mèi mei　Tā jiào Mǎ lì　Tā

e.g. How old is Guóyīng? _____15 years old_____

1. What is his dad called? _____

2. How old is dad? _____

3. How old is mum? _____

4. How many brothers and sisters does he have? _____

29 èrshíjiǔ 二十九

Unit 3

The four different Chinese 'i' tones

Words ending in 'i' in Chinese rhyme with 'bee', except for the special cases of: **chi**, **shi**, **zhi**, **ci**, **si**, **zi**, and **ri**.

Exercise 3.23 - Recognising the 4 different 'i'

Look at the words below and circle the correct tones. You might need to look back at Units 1 and 2 of the textbook/workbook to find your answers. We have completed an example for you.

e.g. li (strength)	1st	2nd	3rd	(4th)
1. ni (you)	1st	2nd	3rd	4th
2. qi (seven)	1st	2nd	3rd	4th
3. nin ('polite' you)	1st	2nd	3rd	4th
4. ji (how many?)	1st	2nd	3rd	4th

Exercise 3.24 - Tones review: Units 1-3

Look at the words below and circle the correct tones. Again, you might need to look back at Units 1 and 2 of the textbook/workbook to find your answers.

1. hao (good)	1st	2nd	3rd	4th
2. jia (home/family)	1st	2nd	3rd	4th
3. sui (age)	1st	2nd	3rd	4th
4. pengyou (friend)	1st	2nd	3rd	4th
5. shi (ten)	1st	2nd	3rd	4th
6. ling (zero)	1st	2nd	3rd	4th

The origins of 好 (good)

The Chinese word, **hǎo**, is made up of two parts – a woman 女 and child 子. The 女 character originated as a picture of a woman sitting on the ground, and the 子 character as a picture of a baby wrapped in a bundle.

Exercise 3.25 - Write 'female', 'son/child' in Chinese characters

First trace over the grey strokes and then complete the <u>full</u> character <u>3 times</u> in the empty boxes.

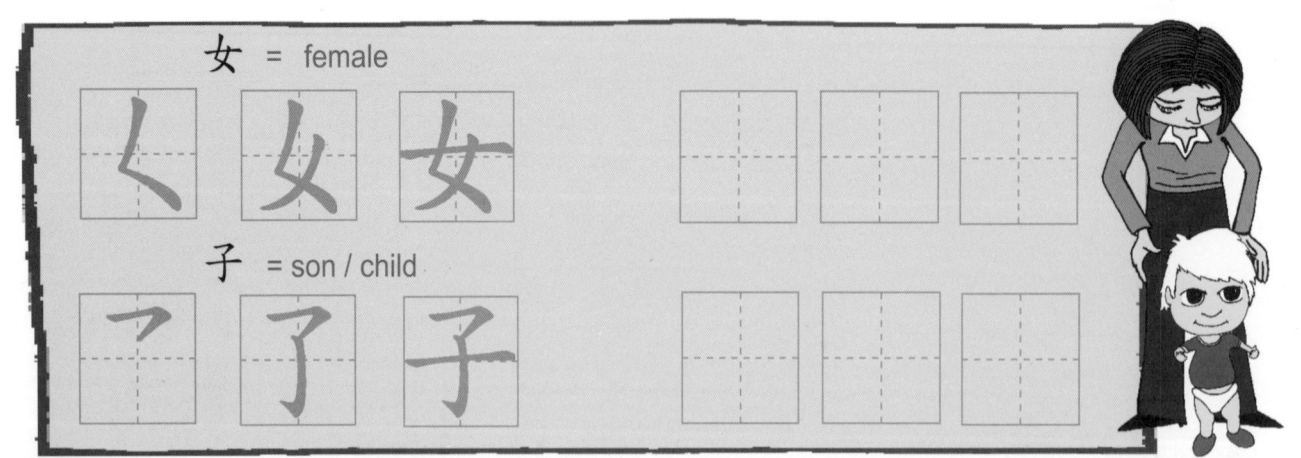

女 = female

子 = son / child

Now complete the Chinese character for 'good' <u>3 times</u> in the empty boxes.

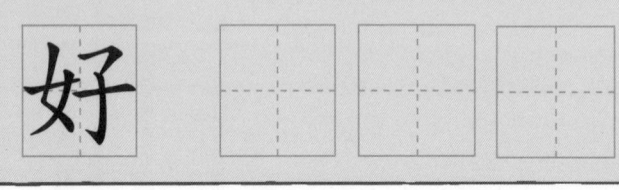

好

30 sānshí 三十

Unit 3

Exercise 3.26 – Testing the characters: 子 女 好
Look at the pinyin text made up of **nǚ**, **zǐ** and **hǎo**. Which set of characters matches the pinyin? We have completed an example for you.

e.g.	hǎo – zǐ – zǐ – hǎo – nǚ – nǚ	1.	zǐ – nǚ – nǚ – hǎo – zǐ – nǚ
a)	好-子-子-女-女-好	a)	子-子-女-好-好-好
b)	好-子-子-女-好-好	b)	子-女-女-好-子-女
c)	(好-子-子-好-女-女)	c)	子-好-好-女-子-女
2.	nǚ – nǚ – zǐ – nǚ – zǐ – hǎo	3.	nǚ – hǎo – hǎo – hǎo – nǚ – zǐ
a)	女-女-子-女-子-好	a)	好-女-子-好-女-子
b)	子-女-好-子-女-好	b)	女-好-好-好-女-子
c)	子-好-女-子-好-女	c)	子-好-女-子-好-女

Exercise 3.27 – How are you? I am very well
Below is a conversation between two people. Read the pinyin and complete all the boxes with the correct Chinese characters. We have completed the first two for you.

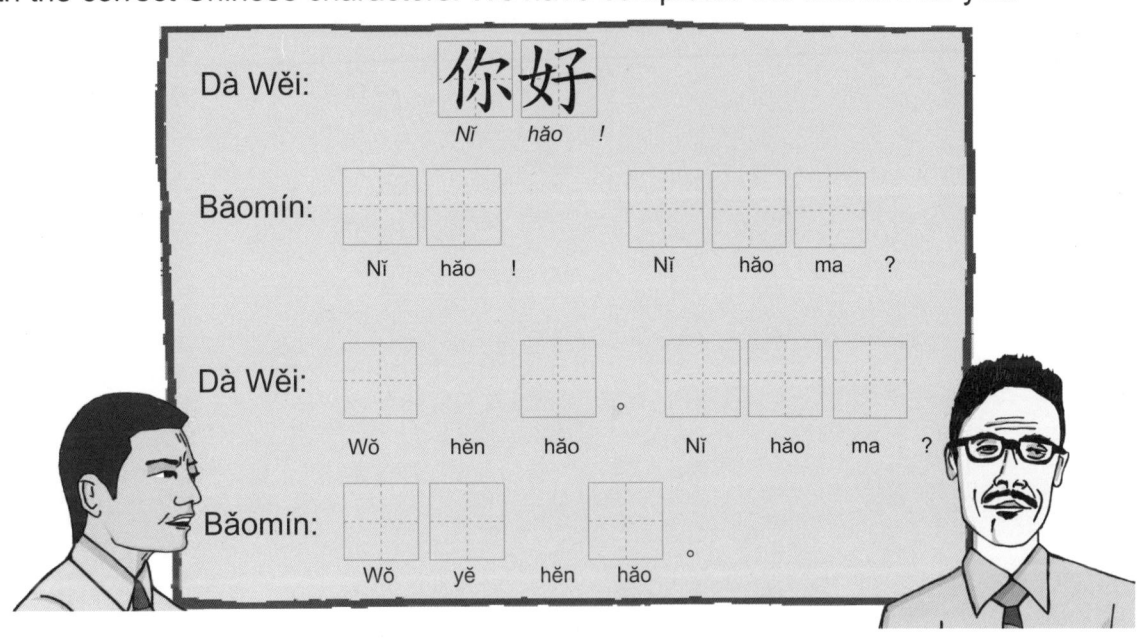

Dà Wěi: 你 好 !
  Nǐ hǎo

Bǎomín: ☐ ☐ !   ☐ ☐ ☐ ?
  Nǐ hǎo   Nǐ hǎo ma

Dà Wěi: ☐ ☐ ☐ 。 ☐ ☐ ☐ ?
  Wǒ hěn hǎo   Nǐ hǎo ma

Bǎomín: ☐ ☐ ☐ ☐ 。
  Wǒ yě hěn hǎo

Animals in China

猫	māo	=	cat
狗	gǒu	=	dog
马	mǎ	=	horse
兔子	tùzi	=	rabbit

课本

Exercise 3.28 – Translation practice
Look at the English sentences on the left and provide the correct translations using Chinese pinyin. We have completed the first one for you.

e.g.	Do you have a dog?	I don't have a dog.
	Nǐ yǒu gǒu ma?	**Wǒ méiyǒu gǒu.**
1.	Does mum have a cat?	Mum has a cat.
	_____?	_____.
2.	Does he have a rabbit?	He doesn't have a rabbit.
	_____?	_____.

31 sānshíyī 三十一

Unit 3

3. Does she have a horse?   She has a horse.
   _____?   _____.

4. Does dad have a cat?   Dad does not have a cat.
   _____?   _____.

Exercise 3.29 – Write 'horse' in Chinese characters
First trace over the grey strokes and then complete the <u>full</u> characters <u>3 times</u> in the empty boxes.

mǎ = horse

フ 马 马

Exercise 3.30 – Does Xiǎojūn have a cat?
Look at the dialogue below between Míngming and Xiǎojūn and then answer the questions below in English in the gaps provided. We have completed an example for you.

Míngming: 你 有 狗 吗 ?
            yǒu gǒu ma

Xiǎojūn: 我 没有 狗。
            méi yǒu gǒu

Míngming: 你 妈妈 有 猫 吗 ?
            mā ma yǒu māo ma

Xiǎojūn: 她 有 猫。
            Tā yǒu māo

Míngming: 你 姐姐 有 猫 吗 ?
            jiě jie yǒu māo ma

Xiǎojūn: 她 没有 猫。
            Tā méi yǒu māo

Míngming: 你 朋友 有 马 吗 ?
            yǒu mǎ ma

Xiǎojūn: 我 不 知道。
            zhī dào

e.g. Does Xiǎojūn *have a dog*?   <u>Xiǎojūn does not have a dog.</u>

1. Which one of Xiǎojūn's relations has a cat? _____

2. Which one of Xiǎojūn's relations does <u>not</u> have a cat? _____

3. Does Xiǎojūn's friend have a horse? _____

32 sānshí'èr 三十二

Food and drink in China

Exercise 3.31 – Questions about Chinese food and drink
What do you remember from Unit 3? Rely on your memory or use the internet to choose the correct answers below! We have completed an example for you.

e.g. What do people in the north of China prefer to eat?
  a) seafood and vegetables ☐
  b) meat, pork, beef and lamb ☑
  c) noodles ☐

1. What do people in the south of China prefer to eat?
   a) seafood, poultry and vegetables ☐
   b) soup and desserts ☐
   c) noodle dishes ☐

2. Which of the following is a famous dish from Sichuan?
   a) spring rolls ☐
   b) beef and bean sprouts ☐
   c) hotpot ☐

3. What should you <u>not</u> do with chopsticks?
   a) use them with your left hand ☐
   b) snap them at the start of a meal ☐
   c) tap your rice bowl with them ☐

4. How many provinces are there in China?
   a) 33 ☐
   b) 50 ☐
   c) 103 ☐

5. What is a popular dish in Héběi province?
   a) dimsum ☐
   b) Peking duck ☐
   c) flatbreads ☐

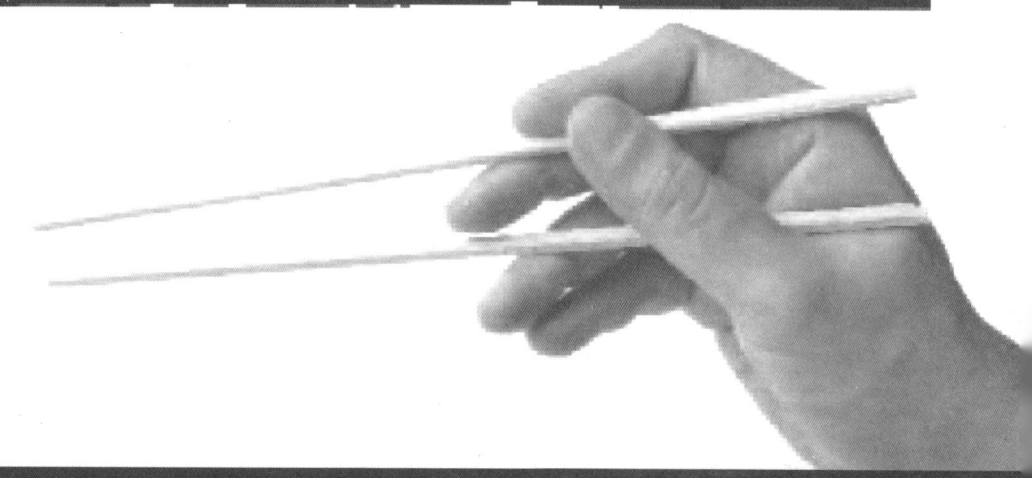

Unit 4

UNIT 4 - MY THINGS

Exercise 4.1 – Do you remember?
Look at the words below and find the translations for things around us. We have completed 'paper' for you.

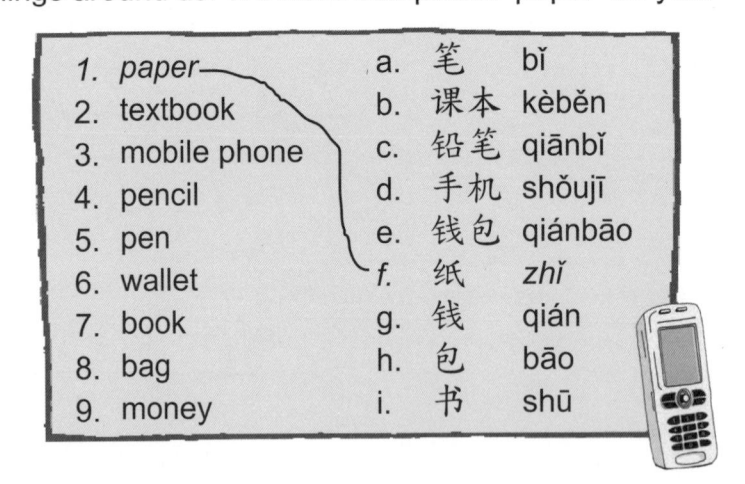

1. paper
2. textbook
3. mobile phone
4. pencil
5. pen
6. wallet
7. book
8. bag
9. money

a. 笔 bǐ
b. 课本 kèběn
c. 铅笔 qiānbǐ
d. 手机 shǒujī
e. 钱包 qiánbāo
f. 纸 zhǐ
g. 钱 qián
h. 包 bāo
i. 书 shū

Exercise 4.2 – My things in my crossword
Fill in the crossword using the key on the right hand side. 1-across has been completed for you.

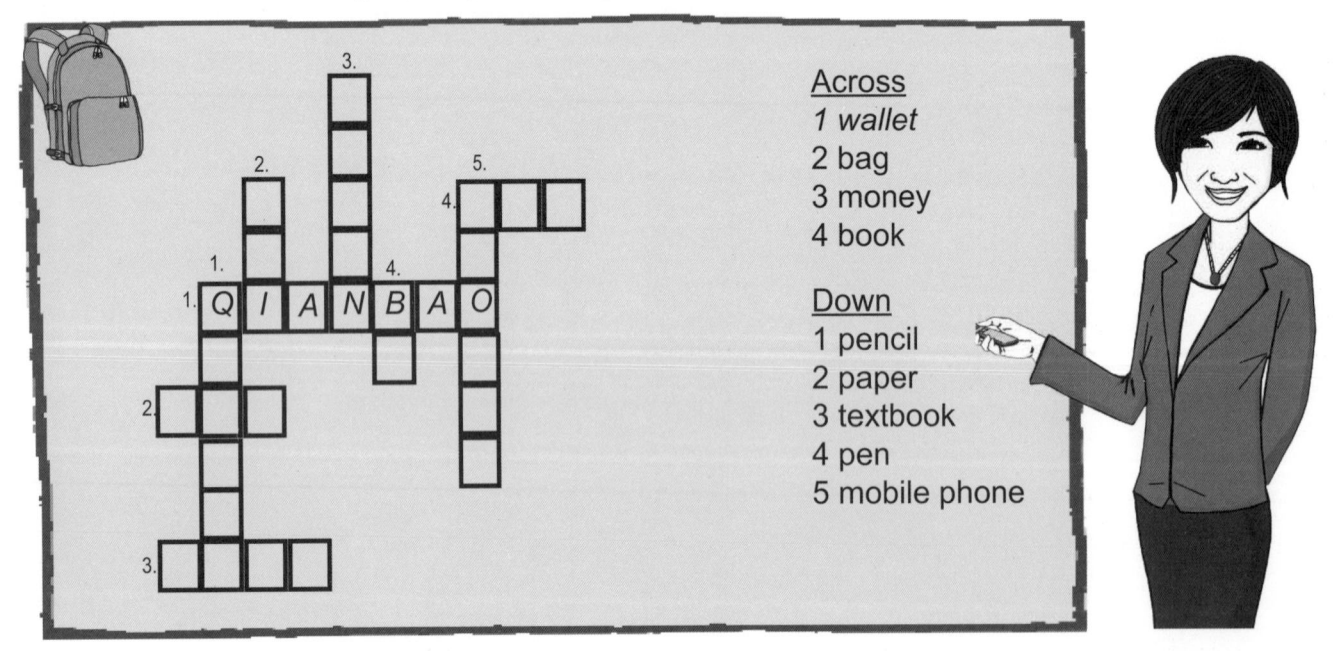

1. Q I A N B A O

Across
1 wallet
2 bag
3 money
4 book

Down
1 pencil
2 paper
3 textbook
4 pen
5 mobile phone

Exercise 4.3 – Review: Do you have or do you not have?
Read the English sentences on the left and translate them into Chinese. We have completed an example for you.

e.g. Do you have a textbook?   Nǐ yǒu kèběn ma?

1. Do you have a wallet?   _____?
2. I don't have a mobile phone.   _____.
3. I have a bag.   _____.
4. I don't have a pen.   _____.
5. Do you have a book?   _____?
6. Do you have a pencil?   _____?

34 sānshísì 三十四

Unit 4

Exercise 4.4 – Write 'book' and 'water' in Chinese characters
First trace over the grey strokes and then complete the full characters 3 times in the empty boxes.

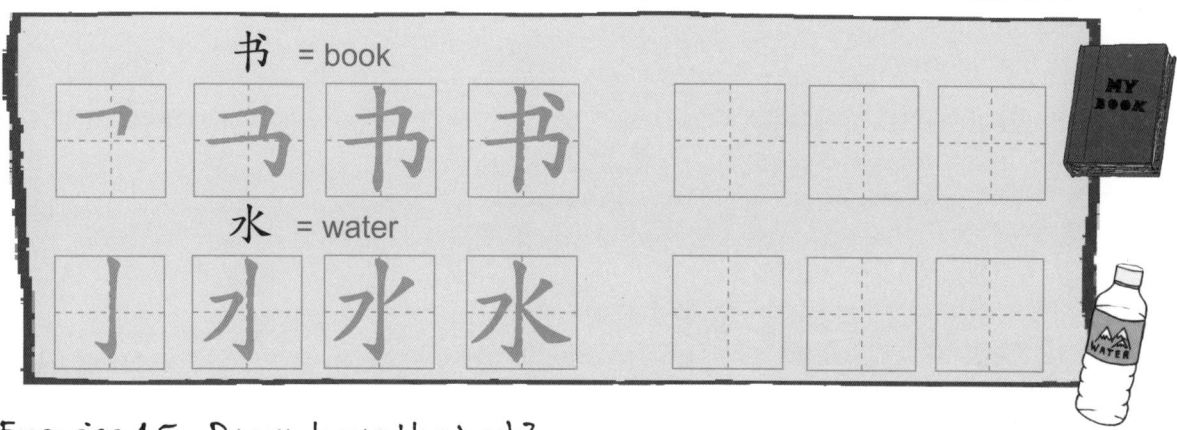

书 = book

水 = water

Exercise 4.5 – Do you have the book?
Look at the questions in English on the left and write the correct translations using Chinese characters on the right. We have completed an example for you.

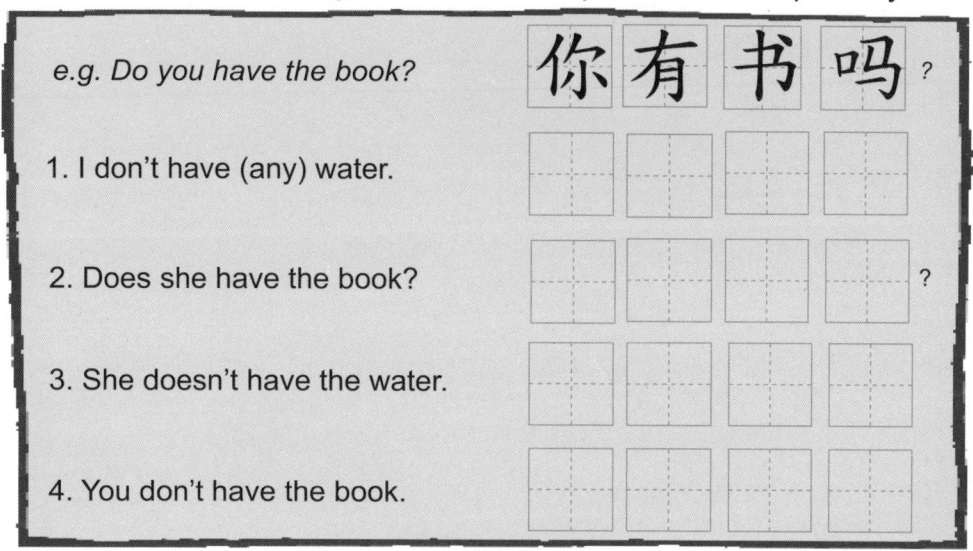

e.g. Do you have the book?   你 有 书 吗 ?

1. I don't have (any) water.

2. Does she have the book?   ?

3. She doesn't have the water.

4. You don't have the book.

What is this?

这是什么	Zhè shì shénme?	=	What is this?
这是。。。	Zhè shì...	=	This is...
这是课本	Zhè shì kèběn.	=	This is a textbook.

课本

Exercise 4.6 – Answer the questions in Chinese
Read the Chinese questions on the left and then answer them in Chinese. We have completed an example for you.

e.g. Zhè shì shénme?   Zhè shì kèběn.

1. Zhè shì shénme?   _____.

2. Zhè shì shénme?   _____.

3. Zhè shì shénme?   _____.

4. Zhè shì shénme?   _____.

35 sānshíwǔ 三十五

Unit 4

Exercise 4.7 - Is this true or false?
Look at the words and accompanying pictures and decide whether the sentence is true or false. <u>If you think the answer is false</u>, you must then write out the <u>correct answer</u> in the space provided to the right. We have completed the first one for you.

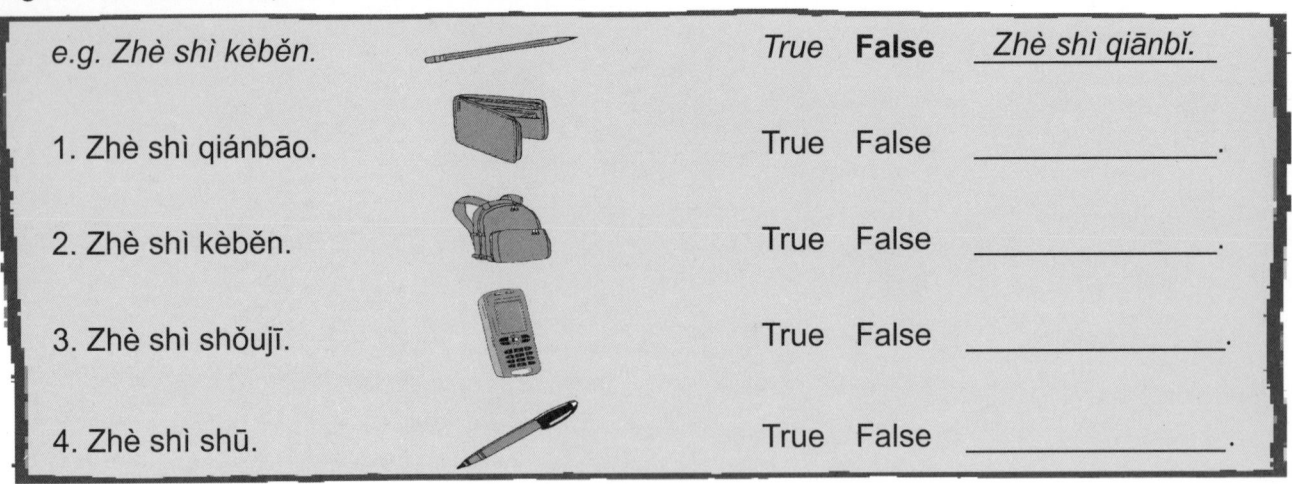

e.g. Zhè shì kèběn.	True **False**	_Zhè shì qiānbǐ._
1. Zhè shì qiánbāo.	True False	_____.
2. Zhè shì kèběn.	True False	_____.
3. Zhè shì shǒujī.	True False	_____.
4. Zhè shì shū.	True False	_____.

Exercise 4.8 - Write 'this' and 'to be' in Chinese characters
First trace over the grey strokes and then complete the <u>full</u> characters <u>3 times</u> in the empty boxes.

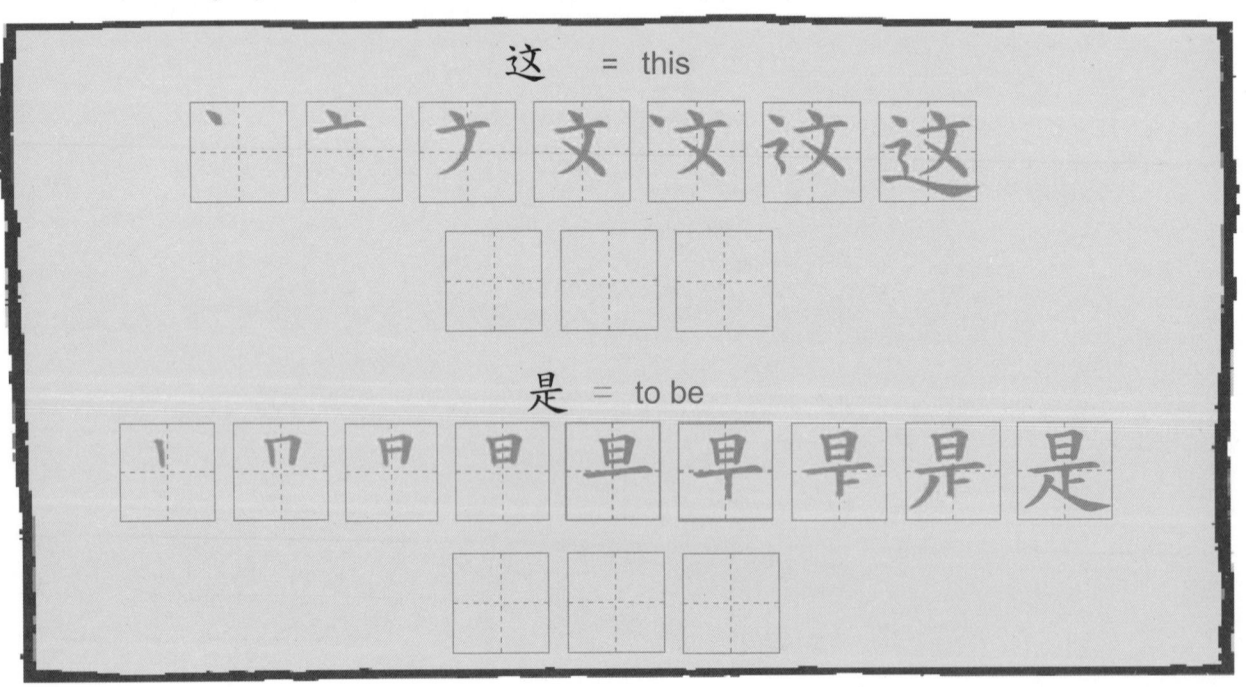

这 = this

是 = to be

Exercise 4.9 - Count how many...
Below is a box containing all the Chinese characters that you have learnt so far. Count <u>how many</u> examples there are of 这 and 是. Make sure you write the number using characters! We have circled a few to get you started.

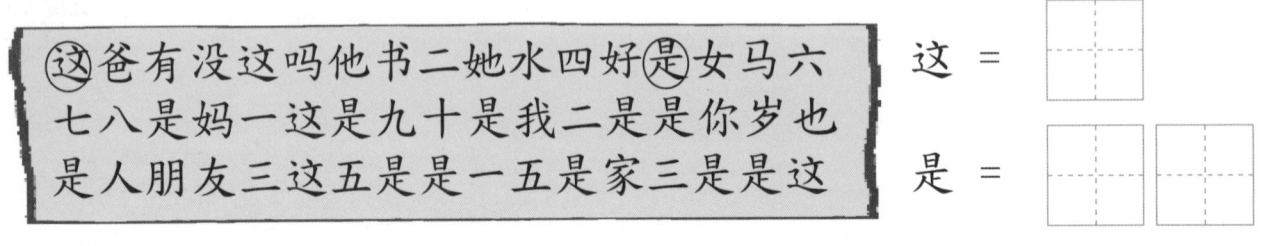

这爸有没这吗他书二她水四好是女马六
七八是妈一这是九十是我二是是你岁也
是人朋友三这五是是一五是家三是是这

这 =

是 =

36 sānshíliù 三十六

Unit 4

Saying negatives in Chinese

不	bù, bú	= not, do not
知道	zhīdào	= to know
这不是	Zhè bú shì...	= This is not...
不知道	bù zhīdào	= to not know

课本

(!) Watch the change in tone from bù to bú in bú shì.

Exercise 4.10 – Sentence match
Match the Chinese sentences to the English sentences. We have completed the first one for you.

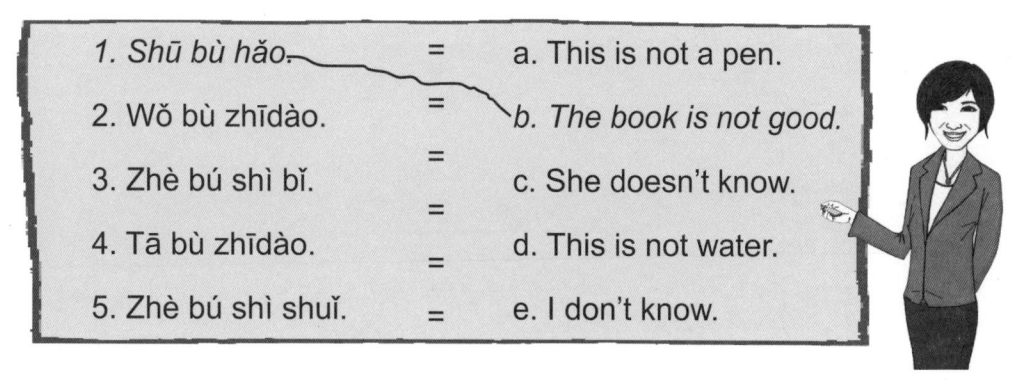

1. Shū bù hǎo.	=	a. This is not a pen.
2. Wǒ bù zhīdào.	=	b. The book is not good.
3. Zhè bú shì bǐ.	=	c. She doesn't know.
4. Tā bù zhīdào.	=	d. This is not water.
5. Zhè bú shì shuǐ.	=	e. I don't know.

Exercise 4.11 – What is this?
Look at the pictures below and complete the dialogues that follow. We have completed an example for you.

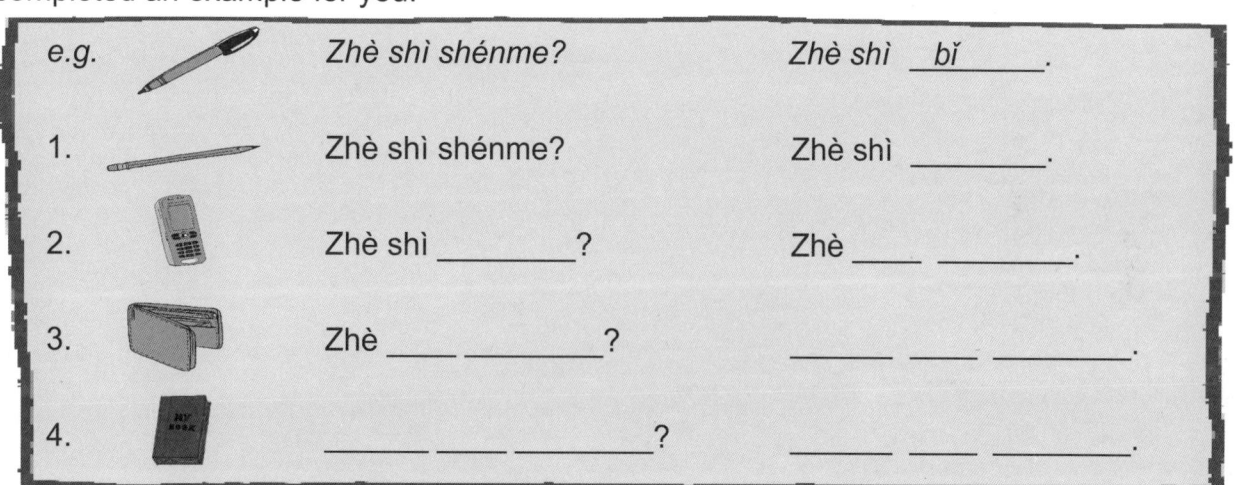

e.g.   Zhè shì shénme?   Zhè shì __bǐ__.

1.   Zhè shì shénme?   Zhè shì _____.

2.   Zhè shì _____?   Zhè ____ _____.

3.   Zhè ____ _____?   ____ ____ _____.

4.   ____ ____ _____?   ____ ____ _____.

Exercise 4.12 – Let's write 'not' and 'what' in Chinese characters
First trace over the grey strokes and then complete the full characters 3 times in the empty boxes.

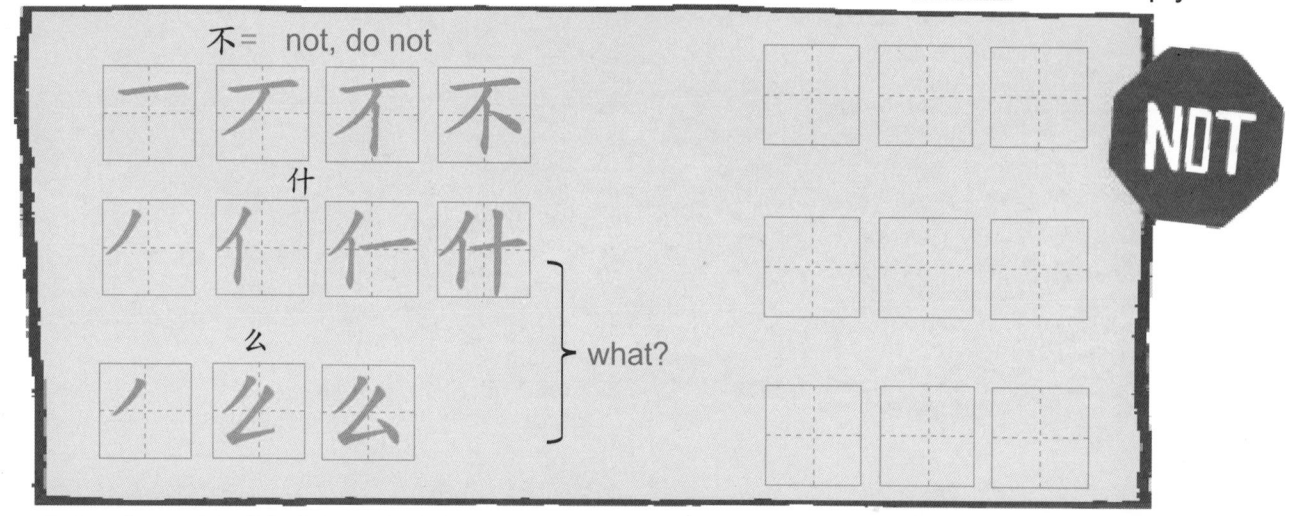

不 = not, do not

什 } what?
么

NOT

37 sānshíqī 三十七

Unit 4

Exercise 4.13 – 这是 and 这不是
On the left are pictures of objects for some words that you have learnt in this unit. First write 'this is not' followed by 'this is', using Chinese characters. Next, you should write the correct pinyin for the pictures in the spaces on the right. We have completed an example for you.

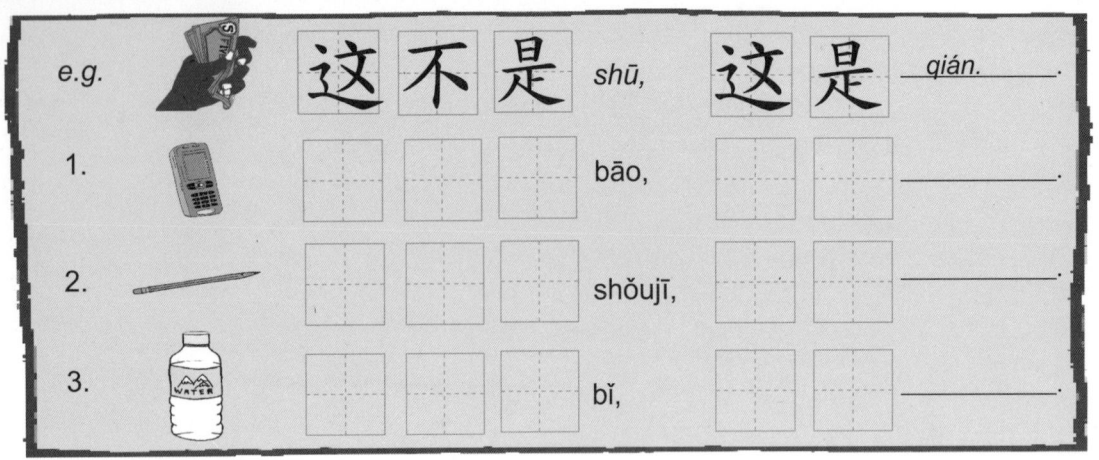

e.g.	这不是 shū,	这是	_qián_.
1.		bāo,	
2.		shǒujī,	
3.		bǐ,	

Exercise 4.14 – What is this?
Look at the pictures below and write the question 'What is this?' in Chinese characters. Then answer each of the questions using characters and pinyin where necessary. We have completed an example for you.

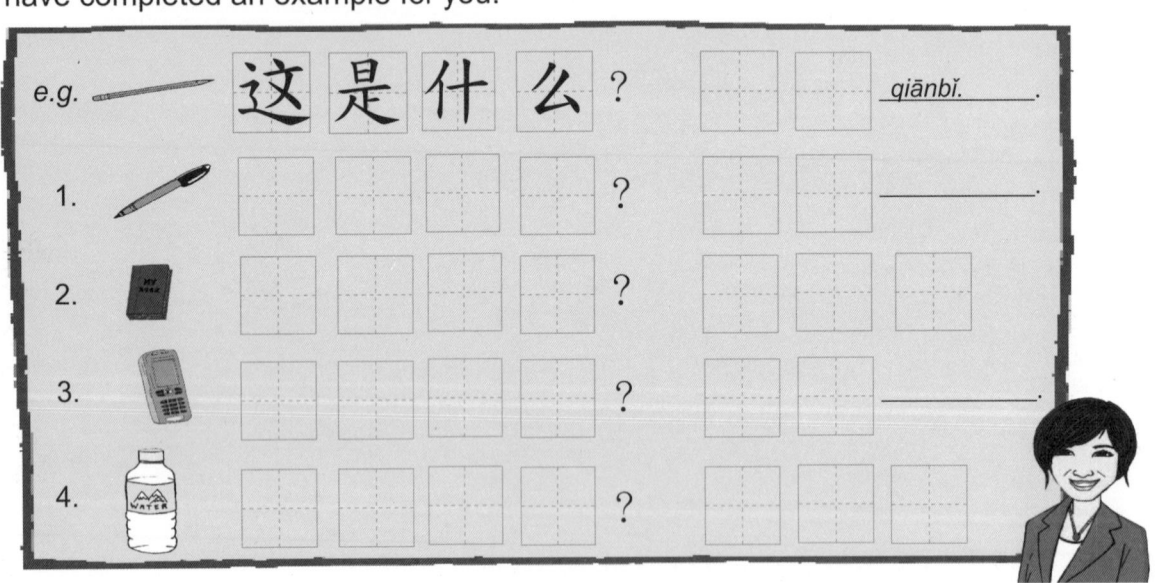

e.g.	这是什么?		_qiānbǐ_.
1.		?	
2.		?	
3.		?	
4.		?	

How do we say 'that' in Chinese

那	Nà	= That
那是	Nà shì...	= That is...
那是笔	Nà shì bǐ.	= That is a pen.

那不是	Nà bú shì...	= That is not...
那不是水	Nà bú shì shuǐ.	= That is not water.
那是什么	Nà shì shénme?	= What is that?

课本

Exercise 4.15 – Translate into Chinese - fill in the gaps
Complete the sentences remembering to use **nà, bù, shì** and **shénme** in the correct places. Remember the tone change on **bù**! We have completed an example for you.

e.g. What is that?	_Nà_ _shì_ _shénme_ ?
1. That is a pen, that is not paper.	____ shì _____, ____ bú shì _____.
2. That is not a bag, that is a wallet.	____ bú shì _____, ____ shì _____.
3. That is not a pencil, that is a book.	____ ____ _____, ____ shì _____.

38 sānshíbā 三十八

Unit 4

Exercise 4.16 – What is that?
Look at the pictures below and complete the dialogues that follow. We have completed an example for you.

e.g.	Nà shì shénme?	Nà shì __shuǐ__.
1.	Nà shì shénme?	Nà shì _____.
2.	Nà shì _____?	Nà _____ _____.
3.	Nà _____ _____?	_____ _____ _____.
4.	_____ _____ _____?	_____ _____ _____.

Exercise 4.17 – Write 'that' in Chinese characters
First trace over the grey strokes and then complete the full characters 3 times in the empty boxes.

那 = that

丁 丬 氵 爿 那 那

Exercise 4.18 – Reading comprehension
Read through the following passage and answer the questions in English. We have completed an example for you.

Mǐn: 那 是 课本
Nà shì kè běn 。

Fāngfang: 我 知 道
zhī dào 。

Mǐn: 那 是 什 么
Nà shì shén me ?

Fāngfang: 我 不 知 道 。 这 是 手 机 吗 ?
bù zhī dào 。 Zhè shì shǒu jī ?

Mǐn: 那 不 是 手 机 。 这 是 钱 包 。
Nà bú shì shǒu jī 。 Zhè shì qián bāo 。

e.g. What is the first object mentioned? — textbook

1. How does Fāngfang reply when asked about it? _____
2. What does Mǐn then ask? _____?
3. What does Fāngfang think it is? _____
4. What is the last object mentioned? _____

39 sānshíjiǔ 三十九

Unit 4

How do we say 'who' in Chinese?

谁	shéi?	= who?
这是谁	zhè shì shéi?	= who is this?
那是谁	nà shì shéi?	= who is that?
你是谁	nǐ shì shéi?	= who are you?
他是谁	tā shì shéi?	= who is he?
她是谁	tā shì shéi?	= who is she?

Exercise 4.19 – Who is that?

The conversation below between Xiǎojūn and Katie has been scrambled. You must write the number next to the sentence to represent its position within the conversation. There are eight sentences in total, including the 2 examples which we have completed for you.

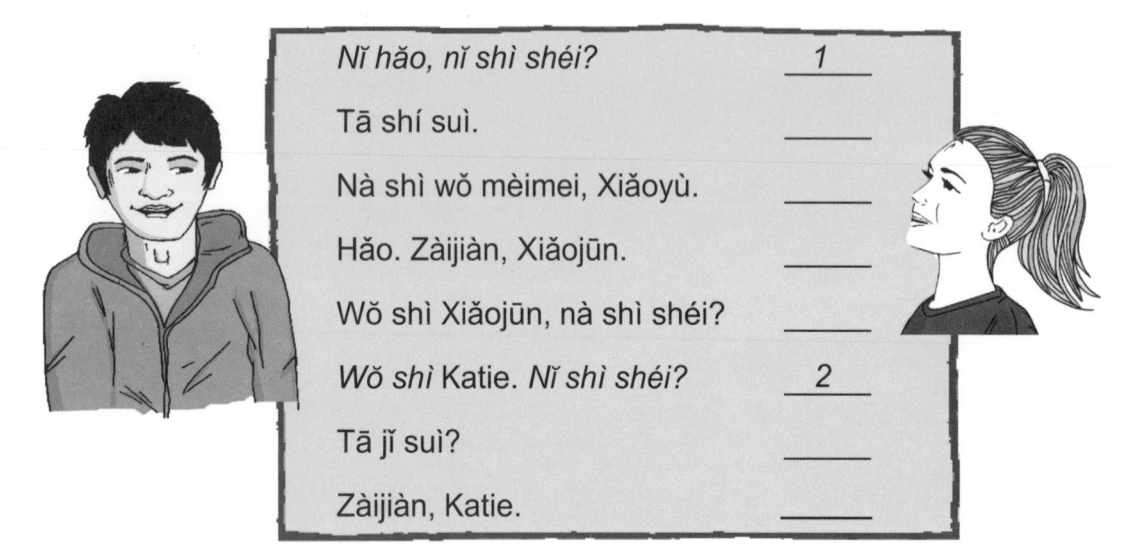

Nǐ hǎo, nǐ shì shéi?	1
Tā shí suì.	___
Nà shì wǒ mèimei, Xiǎoyù.	___
Hǎo. Zàijiàn, Xiǎojūn.	___
Wǒ shì Xiǎojūn, nà shì shéi?	___
Wǒ shì Katie. Nǐ shì shéi?	2
Tā jǐ suì?	___
Zàijiàn, Katie.	___

Exercise 4.20 Writing 'who' in Chinese characters

First trace over the grey strokes and then complete the full characters <u>full</u> characters <u>3 times</u> in the empty boxes.

谁 = who?

Exercise 4.21 – Who are you?

Translate the English questions on the left into Chinese characters. We have completed an example for you.

e.g. Who is she?   她是谁?

1. Who are you?   ___ ___ ___ ?

40 sìshí 四十

Unit 4

2. Who is he? ☐☐☐ ?

3. Who is she? ☐☐☐ ?

How to talk about possessions in Chinese

我的	wǒ de...	= my...
我的家	wǒ de jiā	= my family
你的	nǐ de...	= your...
你的猫	nǐ de māo	= your cat

他的	ta de...	= his
她的书	ta de shū	= her book
爸爸的	baba de...	= dad's...
老师的钱包	lǎoshī de qiánbāo	= teacher's wallet

课本

Exercise 4.22 – Mine, yours, his/hers

Below you will find some short sentences in English. Please use the correct personal pronoun (mine, yours, his/hers) + **de** + the object in question. We have completed an example for you.

e.g. *his pen* ___tā de bǐ___

1. your wallet _____
2. my textbook _____
3. her mobile phone _____
4. your book _____
5. his book _____

Below you will find some short sentences in English. Please use the correct family name + **de** + the object in question. We have completed an example for you.

e.g. *younger brother's pencil* ___dìdi de qiānbǐ___

1. older sister's paper _____
2. dad's mobile phone _____
3. older brother's water _____
4. younger brother's pen _____
5. mum's wallet _____

Exercise 4.23 – Writing de in Chinese characters

First trace over the grey strokes and then complete the <u>full</u> characters <u>3 times</u> in the empty boxes.

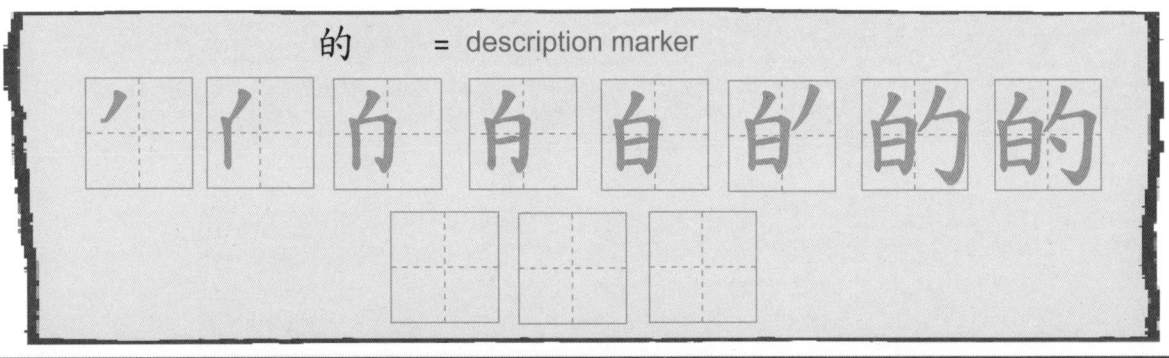

的 = description marker

ノ 亻 冇 白 白 白 的 的

41 sìshíyī 四十一

Unit 4

Exercise 4.24 – Practise writing *de* in Chinese sentences
Translate the short sentences into Chinese characters and/or pinyin in the grids and blanks provided. We have completed an example for you.

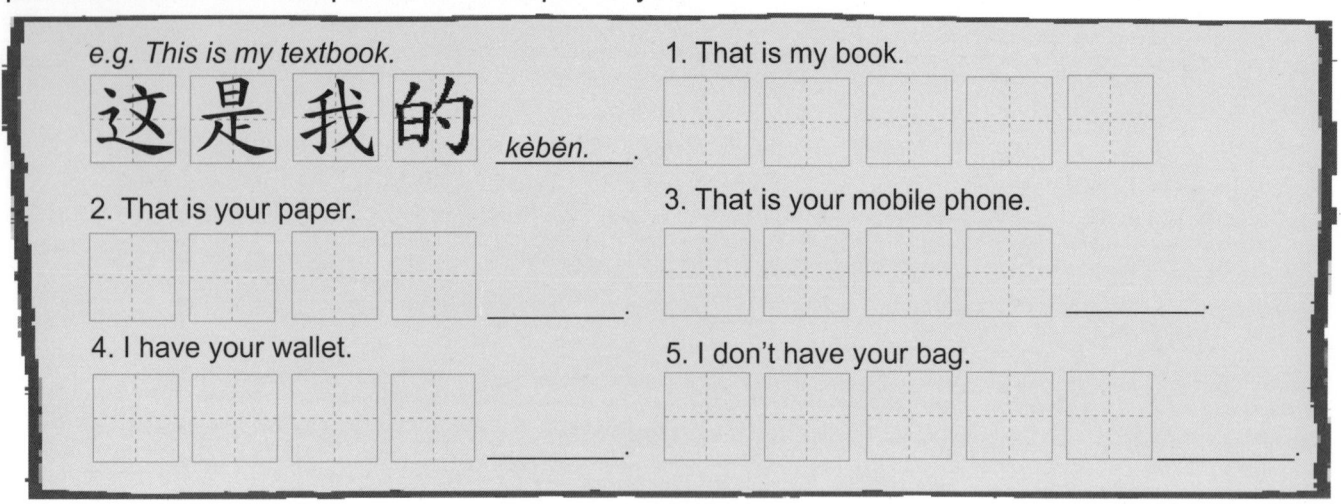

e.g. *This is my textbook.*
这 是 我 的 *kèběn*.

1. That is my book.

2. That is your paper.

3. That is your mobile phone.

4. I have your wallet.

5. I don't have your bag.

The origins of 水 (water)

课本

The character for water (水) originally looked like a flowing river. When it appears as a component of other characters it usually changes form and becomes three drops (氵).

Exercise 4.25 – Count how many...
Below is a box containing lots of different Chinese characters that you have already learnt. Count <u>how many</u> examples there are of 水. Make sure you write the number using characters! We have circled one of them to to get you started.

㊄书有吗那吗他书二她水弟水是女四八
的七是爸四一这是岁十我我二朋有哥岁
没是人有友水谁五是一哥水家水是第你

水 =

Exercise 4.26 – Water, water everywhere
Read the English sentences and complete the boxes with the correct Chinese characters – and be careful of all the water! We have completed an example for you.

e.g. What is this?   这 是 什 么 ?

1. This is water.

2. What is that? ?

3. That is also water.

4. I have water.

5. I don't have water.

42 *sìshí'èr* 四十二

Unit 4

The four different Chinese 'o' tones.

Words ending in 'o' and 'uo' sound quite similar in Chinese, and are similar to an English 'or' but are made with more rounded lips.

Exercise 4.27 - Recognising the 4 different 'o' tones
The grid below contains the 'o' sound pinyin words with different tones. You must find the matching tones in the grid for each of the four words. We have completed an example fo you.

e.g. bo (1st tone)

1. fo (2nd tone)
2. duo (1st tone)
3. po (4th tone)
4. wo (3rd tone)
5. lo (no tone)

duó	bō	duò
fò	wò	lo
duò	pǒ	fò
wō	fó	pó
pǒ	duó	duò
duǒ	wō	fō
fǒ	pǒ	duō
wǒ	pò	pǒ
duó	wò	fò

Practising Chinese Calligraphy

Exercise 4.28 - Calligraphy link
Below you find some examples of Chinese calligraphy in the top row. Draw a line to link the calligraphy to the most likely Chinese characters in the bottom row. We have completed the the first one for you i.e. the answer is 1d.

① 另 ② 出 ③ 奇 ④ 刻 ⑤ 至 ⑥ 意 ⑦ 勝

a 出　b 创　c 意　d 另　e 奇　f 至　g 胜

Exercise 4.29 - Your turn!
Use your answers in Exercise 4.28 to write the corresponding Chinese characters in the character grids below. We have completed the first one for you.

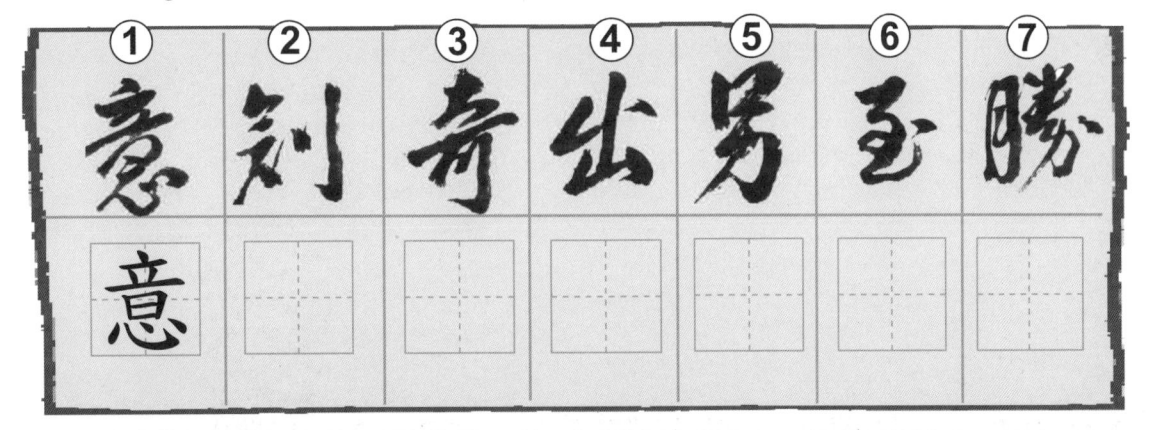

① 意 ② 刻 ③ 奇 ④ 出 ⑤ 另 ⑥ 至 ⑦ 勝

意

UNIT 5 - SHOPPING IN CHINA

How many?

多少 Duōshǎo   =   How many/much?

Duōshǎo is only used when asking questions about numbers <u>above 10</u>. For questions about smaller numbers (for example, how many brothers do you have?), you have to use the word **jǐ**.

Exercise 5.1 - How many?
Match each of the sentences (written in pinyin) on the left to the correct English translations on the right. We have completed the first one for you i.e. answer = *1e*

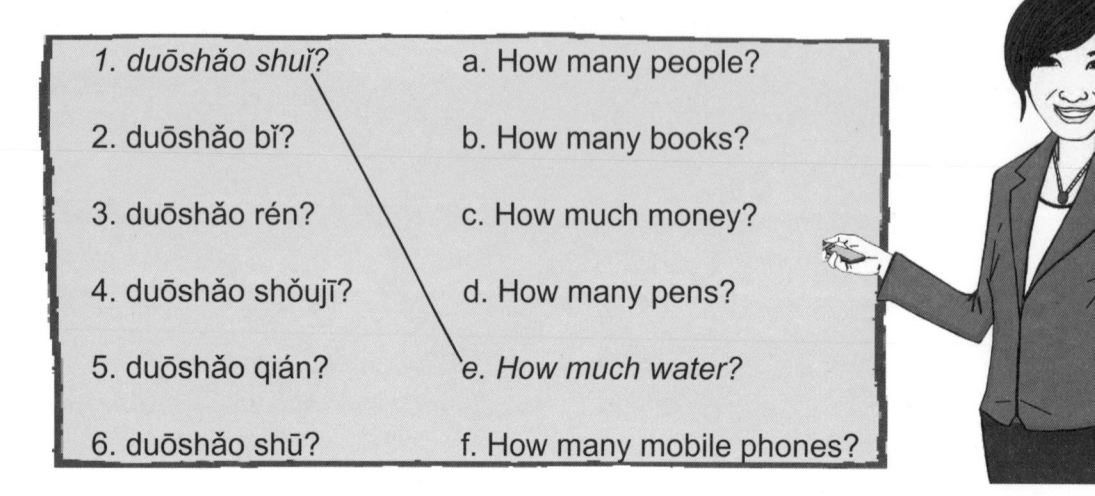

1. duōshǎo shuǐ?	a. How many people?
2. duōshǎo bǐ?	b. How many books?
3. duōshǎo rén?	c. How much money?
4. duōshǎo shǒujī?	d. How many pens?
5. duōshǎo qián?	e. *How much water?*
6. duōshǎo shū?	f. How many mobile phones?

Exercise 5.2 - How many?
Decide if the Chinese characters are the correct characters used for the numbers in brackets on the left hand side. Either tick the 'true' box and copy what you see or tick the 'false' box and write the correct characters. We have completed an example for you.

	Characters	True/False	Your answer
e.g. Duōshǎo? (31)	三 十 九	True ☐ False ☑	三 十 一
1. Duōshǎo? (48)	八 十 四	True ☐ False ☐	
2. Duōshǎo? (77)	七 十 七	True ☐ False ☐	
3. Duōshǎo? (16)	六 十	True ☐ False ☐	
4. Duōshǎo? (93)	九 十 三	True ☐ False ☐	
5. Duōshǎo? (25)	二 十 五	True ☐ False ☐	

44 sìshísì 四十四

Unit 5

Practising prices and Chinese currency

多少钱	Duōshǎo qián?	=	How much is it?
元	Yuán	=	Chinese currency
块	kuài	=	common word for Chinese currency, 'Yuan'

Exercise 5.3 – Practise using duōshǎo qián in practical situations
Look at the the English questions/sentences on the left and then translate them into Chinese pinyin, ensuring that you fill in the gaps. We have completed the first one for you.

Xiǎojūn:	What is that?	___Nà___ shì _shénme_?
Shopkeeper:	That is a mobile phone.	_____ shì _____.
Xiǎojūn:	**How much is it?**	_____ _____?
Shopkeeper:	99 kuai.	_____ _____ _____ kuài.
Xiǎojūn:	What is this?	_____ shì _____?
Shopkeeper:	This is a wallet.	_____ _____ _____.
Xiǎojūn:	**How much is it?**	_____ _____?
Shopkeeper:	31 kuai.	_____ _____ kuài.
Xiǎojūn:	Thank you. Goodbye.	Xièxie. _____.

Exercise 5.4 – Writing Yuan in Chinese characters
First trace over the grey strokes and then complete the full characters 3 times in the empty boxes.

元 Yuan

Exercise 5.5 – How much is that?
For each of the items shown below, complete the questions and answers using pinyin and Chinese characters where necessary. We have completed an example for you.

e.g. Duōshǎo qián?   6 Yuán   六 元

1. Duōshǎo _____?   17 Yuán

2. _____ qián?   60 Yuán

3. _____?   33 Yuán

4. _____?   74 Yuán

45 sìshíwǔ 四十五

Unit 5

Exercise 5.6 - The shopping list

Below is a list of items and how much they cost in 元. Look carefully at the short questions and answer them in <u>English</u>. We have completed an example for you.

Prices

bǐ	五元
kèběn	十一元
shǒujī	七十元
qiānbǐ	四元
shuǐ	三元
qiánbāo	四十六元
zhǐ	八元
bāo	五十元
shū	二十七元

e.g. William bought a textbook and a mobile phone. How much did he spend? __81 Yuan__

1. Mǐn bought a bag and a pencil. How much did he spend? _____

2. Jìng bought a book and a pen. How much did she spend? _____

3. Shū bought some paper and some water. How much did she spend? _____

4. Dàwěi bought a wallet and book. How much did he spend? _____

More useful shopping words

电池	diànchí	=	battery
冰淇淋	bīngqílín	=	ice cream
报纸	bàozhǐ	=	newspaper

Exercise 5.7 - Word Match

Look at the words below and draw a line from the English to the Chinese and the Chinese to the English. We have completed 'textbook' for you.

①
1. textbook — c. kèběn
2. newspaper
3. ice cream
4. wallet
5. pencil
6. paper

a. qiánbāo
b. bàozhǐ
c. kèběn
d. bīngqílín
e. zhǐ
f. qiānbǐ

②
1. shuǐ
2. shǒujī
3. diànchí
4. bāo
5. bǐ
6. liù

a. water
b. bag
c. pen
d. six
e. mobile phone
f. battery

Exercise 5.8 - Translations

Look at the English sentences on the left and translate them into Chinese pinyin in the gaps on the right. We have completed an example for you.

e.g. Do you have ice cream?   Nǐ yǒu bīngqílín ma?

1. I don't have batteries. _____.

2. I have a newspaper. _____.

3. This is not a wallet. _____.

4. Is that a textbook? _____?

46 sìshíliù 四十六

Unit 5

Exercise 5.9 – What do you have in your shop?
Look at the dialogue below between Guóyīng and the shopkeeper and answer the questions below in English. We have completed an example for you.

Guóyīng: 你 有 笔 吗？
           bǐ

Shopkeeper: 有。

Guóyīng: 多少 钱？
         Duō shǎo qián

Shopkeeper: 六 块。
                kuài

Guóyīng: 你 有 报纸 吗？
                 bào zhǐ

Shopkeeper: 有。

Guóyīng: 多少 钱？
         Duō shǎo qián

Shopkeeper: 十三 块。
                  kuài

Guóyīng: 你 有 冰淇淋 吗？
                 bīng qí lín

Shopkeeper: 没有。

Guóyīng: 你 有 电池 吗？
                 diàn chí

Shopkeeper: 有。

Guóyīng: 多少 钱 ？
         Duō shǎo qián

Shopkeeper: 二十五 块
                   kuài

Guóyīng: 谢谢 。
         Xiè xie

e.g. Do they sell pens?   Yes _____

1. How much are the pens?   _____

2. How much are the newspapers?   _____

3. Do they sell ice cream?   _____

4. How much are the batteries?   _____

47 sìshíqī 四十七

Unit 5

Buying things in China

买	mǎi	=	to buy
个	gè	=	measure word
这个	zhè gè	=	this one
那个	nà gè	=	that one

课本

Exercise 5.10 – What is he buying?

Looking at the names of the people below, complete the sentences by asking 'who is buying what?' and then state which person buys which object. We have completed an example for you.

Bǎomín	Míngming	Katie	Xiǎojūn	Chénchen
batteries	ice cream	newspaper	wallet	mobile phone

e.g. Bǎomín mǎi shénme?   *Bǎomín mǎi diànchí.*

1. Míngming mǎi shénme?   _____.

2. Xiǎojūn _____ _____ ?   _____.

3. Katie _____ _____ ?   _____.

4. Chénchen _____ _____ ?   _____.

Exercise 5.11 – Quick search – this and that

Look at the sentences below and circle the correct pinyin to mean 'this' or 'that'. You must look out for not only the correct spelling but also the correct <u>tones</u>. We have completed an example for you.

e.g.	That	nǎ gè àn gè zhè gè (nà gè) zhè gè nā gè
1.	This	zhè gē zhe gè zhè gè zèh gè zhè èg
2.	That	nā gè nà gà ná gè nà gè nǎ gè nà gē
3.	This	zhà gè zhè gè zhě gè zhè gě zhē gè zhè gé

Exercise 5.12 – Write gè in Chinese characters

First trace over the grey strokes and then complete the <u>full</u> characters <u>3 times</u> in the empty boxes.

个 = measure word

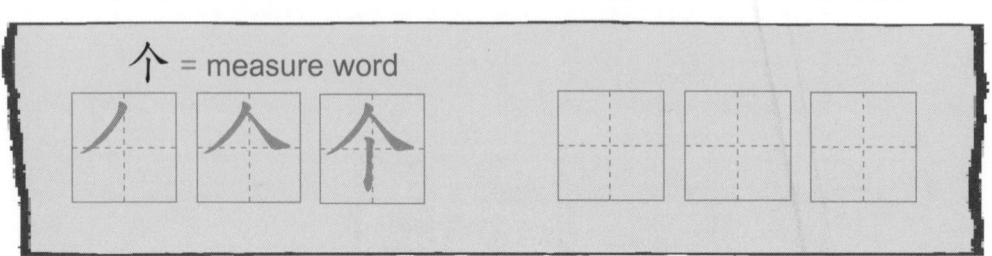

48 sìshíbā 四十八

Unit 5

Exercise 5.13 – What's your friend buying?
Read through the text below and answer the questions in English. We have completed an example for you.

Katie: 你 的 朋友 买 什么？ 　　　　　　　　　mǎi	e.g. What does Jìng's friend buy? _ice cream_
Jìng: 我 的 朋友 买 冰淇淋。 　　　　　　　mǎi　bīng qí lín	1. How much does ice cream cost?
Katie: 多少 钱？ 　　 Duō shǎo qián	
Jìng: 七 元。 　　　 Yuán	2. What does Katie's friend buy?
Katie: 我 的 朋友 买 电池。 　　　　　　　mǎi diàn chí	
Jìng: 多少 钱？ 　　 Duō shǎo qián	3. How much is this item?
Katie: 二十二 元。 　　　　　Yuan	
Jìng: 敏 的 朋友 买 什么？ 　　 Mǐn　　　　　mǎi	4. What does Mǐn's friend buy?
Katie: 他 的 朋友 买 报纸。 　　　　　　　mǎi bào zhǐ	

Exercise 5.14 – How much is this?
Below you will find 4 objects and their prices; 2 are close (next to the person) and 3 are further away (on the table). If an object is close by, we say **zhè gè** (to emphasise 'this'); and if the object is far away, we say **nà gè** (to emphasise 'that'). Now complete the correct Chinese characters for 'this' or 'that' and the price in the boxes provided. We have completed an example for you.

e.g. bag - 那 个 三 十 元

shǒujī — 74 Yuán
bàozhǐ — 11 Yuán
bāo — 30 Yuán
bīngqílín — 8 Yuán

1. newspaper
2. mobile phone
3. ice cream

Unit 5

The importance of hěn in Chinese

很	hěn	=	very
好	hǎo	=	good, nice, OK
大	dà	=	big
小	xiǎo	=	small
贵	guì	=	expensive

课本

Exercise 5.15 – It is very….

For each object below, you must circle the <u>most appropriate</u> description in pinyin using **hěn hǎo, hěn dà, hěn xiǎo** and **hěn guì.** We have completed an example for you.

e.g. a giraffe:	hěn guì	(hěn dà)
1. a mouse:	hěn hǎo	hěn xiǎo
2. an elephant:	hěn xiǎo	hěn dà
3. a new sports car:	hěn xiǎo	hěn guì
4. a sports stadium:	hěn dà	hěn xiǎo
5. a bunch of flowers:	hěn hǎo	hěn xiǎo

Exercise 5.16 – It is not,……

For each of the objects below, you must circle the <u>most appropriate</u> description in pinyin using **bù hǎo, bú dà, bù xiǎo** and **bú guì.** Remember that if **bù** is followed by a <u>4th tone</u> adjective, **bù** becomes <u>2nd tone</u>. For example: **Nà gè bú dà** = That one is not big. We have completed an example for you.

e.g. An oil tanker:	bú dà	(bù xiǎo)
1. A bowl of rice:	bù hǎo	bú guì
2. A bad school grade:	bú xiǎo	bù hǎo
3. A bottle of water:	bú guì	bù hǎo
4. A can of Coca-cola:	bú dà	bù xiǎo
5. A jumbo jet	bù xiǎo	bú dà

Exercise 5.17 – Write 'very', 'big' and 'small' in Chinese characters

First trace over the grey strokes and then complete the <u>full</u> characters <u>3 times</u> in the empty boxes.

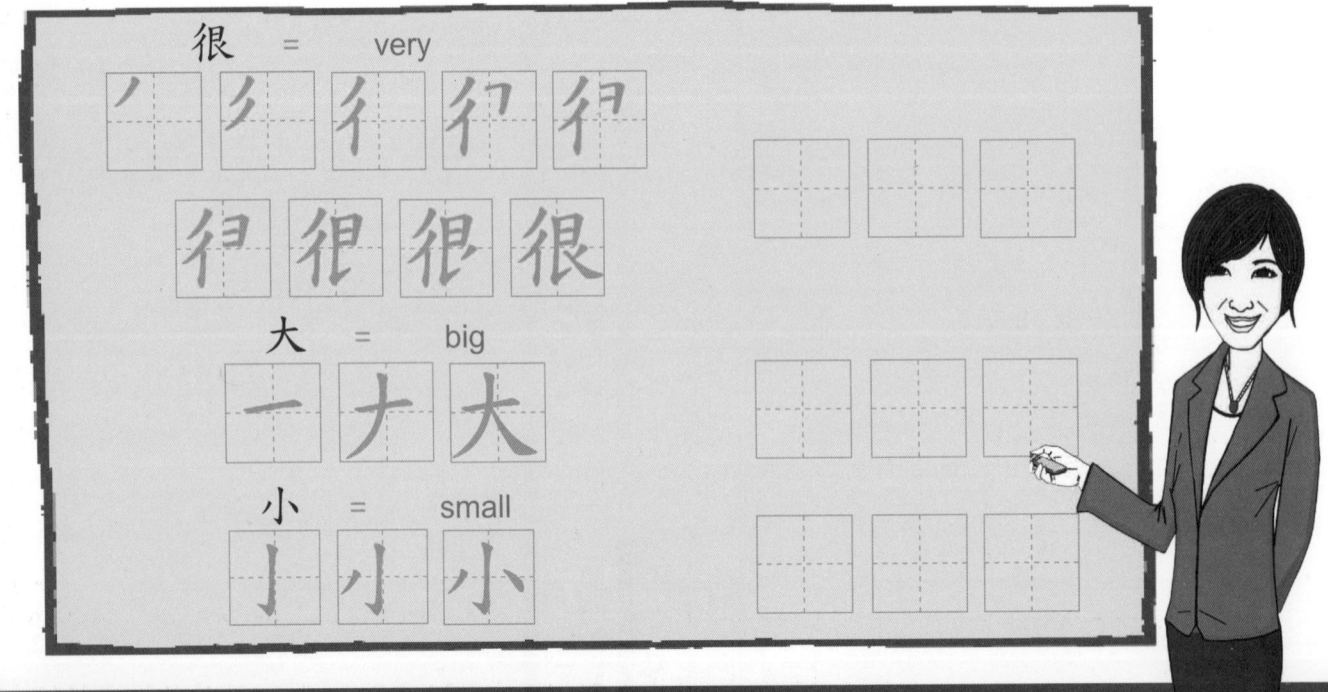

很 = very

大 = big

小 = small

50 wǔshí 五十

Unit 5

Exercise 5.18 - Writing the correct characters

For each object below, write the most appropriate description in Chinese characters using 很大 and 很小. We have completed an example for you.

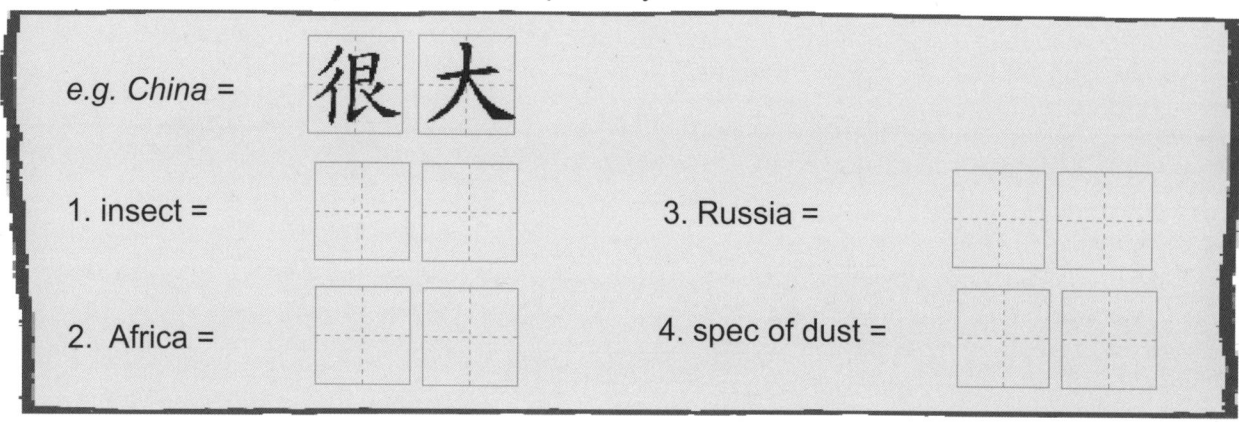

e.g. China = 很大

1. insect =
2. Africa =
3. Russia =
4. spec of dust =

Exercise 5.19 - Revising 不

For each object below, write the most appropriate description in Chinese characters using 不大 and 不小. We have completed an example for you.

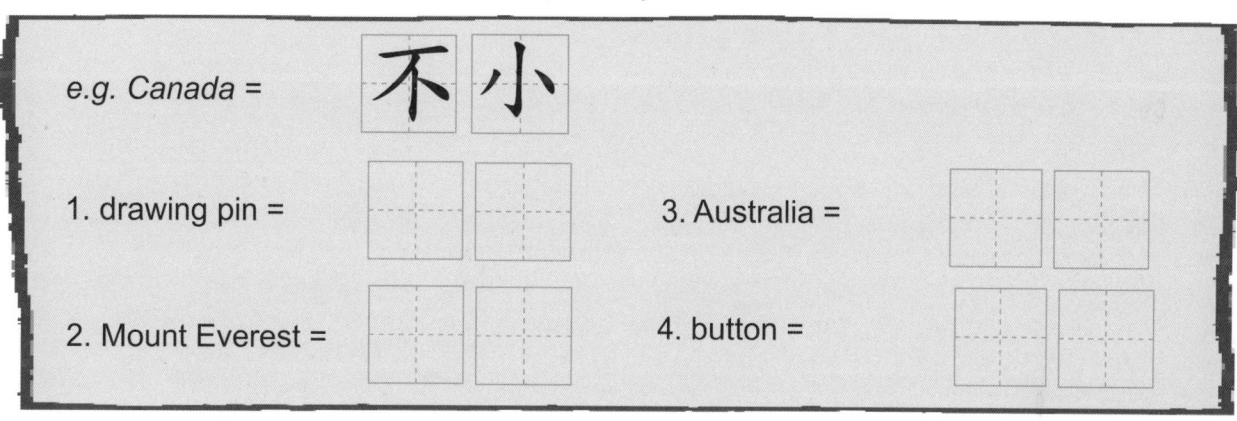

e.g. Canada = 不小

1. drawing pin =
2. Mount Everest =
3. Australia =
4. button =

Exercise 5.20 - This/that is/is not... - Character test

Look at the English sentences below and choose the correct translation out of each of the four options in the exercises below. We have completed an example for you.

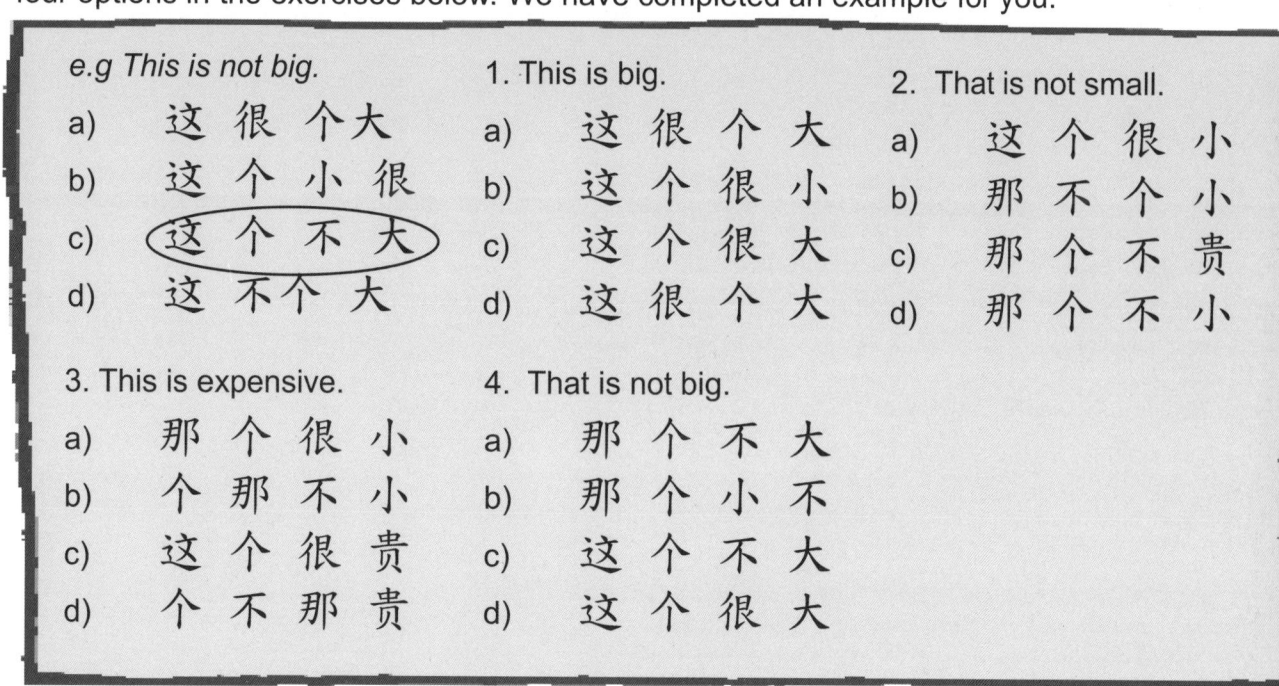

e.g This is not big.
a) 这 很 个 大
b) 这 个 小 很
c) 这 个 不 大 *(circled)*
d) 这 不 个 大

1. This is big.
a) 这 很 个 大
b) 这 个 很 小
c) 这 个 很 大
d) 这 很 个 大

2. That is not small.
a) 这 个 很 小
b) 那 不 个 小
c) 那 个 不 贵
d) 那 个 不 小

3. This is expensive.
a) 那 个 很 小
b) 个 那 不 小
c) 这 个 很 贵
d) 个 不 那 贵

4. That is not big.
a) 那 个 不 大
b) 那 个 小 不
c) 这 个 不 大
d) 这 个 很 大

51 wǔshíyī 五十一

Unit 5

Exercise 5.21 – What does she buy?

Read through the passage below between Shū and the shopkeeper and answer the questions in English in the gaps provided below the dialogue. We have completed an example for you.

Shū: 你 好。

Shopkeeper: 你 好。你 买 什么？
　　　　　　　　　　mǎi

Shū: 你 有 报纸 吗？
　　　　　　bào zhǐ

Shopkeeper: 没有。

Shū: 你 有 铅笔 吗？
　　　　　　qiān bǐ

Shopkeeper: 有。

Shū: 这 个 不 好，这 个 很 小。
　　　　gè　　　　　　gè　hěn　xiǎo

Shopkeeper: 那 个 很 好。
　　　　　　gè　hěn

Shū: 我 买 那 个。多少 钱？
　　　　mǎi　　gè　Duō shǎo qián

Shopkeeper: 十二 元。你 也 买 纸 吗？
　　　　　　Yuán　　　　mǎi zhǐ

Shū: 我 也 买。多少 钱？
　　　mǎi　Duō shǎo qián

Shopkeeper: 二十五 元。
　　　　　　　Yuán

Shū: 好，再见。
　　　　zài jiàn

Shopkeeper: 谢谢，再见。
　　　　　　Xiè xie　zài jiàn

e.g What is the first thing Shū asks for? _a newspaper_

1. What is the second thing Shū asks for? _____
2. How much is it? _____
3. What does she also buy? _____
4. How much does she spend altogether? _____

52 wǔshí'èr 五十二

Unit 5

Exercise 5.22 – Write the 4 elements in Chinese characters
First trace over the grey strokes and then complete the full characters 3 times in the empty boxes.

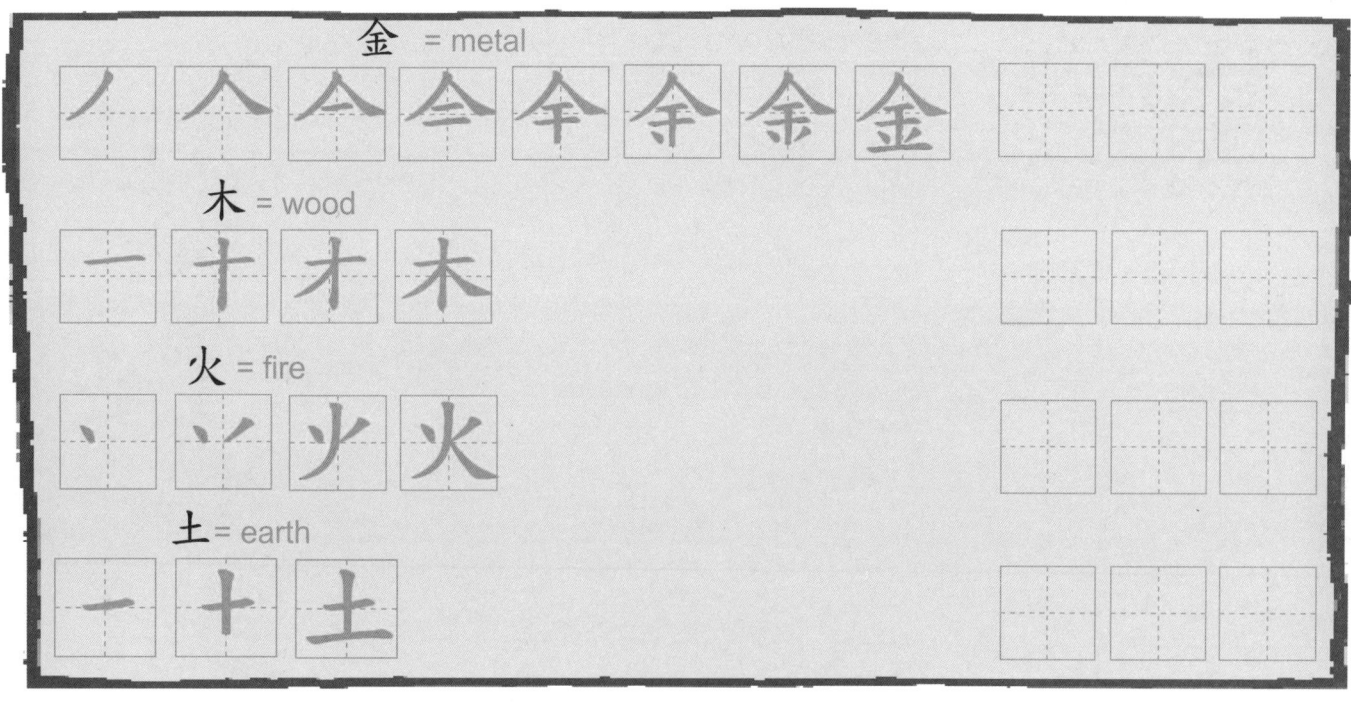

金 = metal

木 = wood

火 = fire

土 = earth

Exercise 5.23 – Amazing characters
Below are the five elements characters: metal, wood, water, fire, and earth.
You must link all the 5 different element character to the characters below where you see one of the elements written. We have completed an example for you.

金　木　水　火　土

鉴 杏 地 李 灯 灰 在 銮 沓 去 堡

Exercise 5.24 – Recognising the 4 different 'u' tones
Each of the text strings below contains the 'u' sound in pinyin words with different tones. For each of the 4 numbered tones on the left, circle the correct matching words. We have completed the first one for you.

1st tone – ū	flat tone	e.g. chū – to exit
2nd tone – ú	rising tone	e.g. hú – lake
3rd tone – ǔ	low tone	e.g. tǔ – ground, earth
4th tone – ù	falling tone	e.g. shù – tree

1st tone: chūchŭchūchŭchùchūchŭchūchŭchūchŭchūchŭchùchūchŭchūchùchūchŭchùchū

2nd tone: húhŭhúhŭhūhúhŭhúhŭhúhŭhūhŭhūhúhŭhūhŭhúhŭhúhŭhúhŭhūhŭhūhŭhúhŭhūhúhŭhŭ

3rd tone: tŭtūtŭtūtŭtūtŭtūtŭtūtŭtūtŭtūtútŭtūtŭtūtŭtūtŭtūtŭtūtŭtūtŭtūtútŭtūtŭtūtŭtūtŭtūtŭ

4th tone: shùshùshúshùshŭshùshŭshúshùshŭshùshūshùshúshùshŭshùshūshùshūshùshŭshùshù.

53 wǔshísān 五十三

Unit 5

Great things to buy in China!

Exercise 5.25 – What's for sale?

What do you remember from Unit 5? Rely on your memory or use the internet to choose the correct answers below! We have completed an example for you.

e.g. When going to buy something in China, there are

a) only a few shops to choose from.
b) lots of different shops to choose from. ✓
c) only online stores to choose from.

1. In a typical Chinese supermarket….

a) entire aisles can be devoted to peanut oil, frozen dumplings or soya sauce.
b) there is no western food.
c) you can only pay with a credit card.

2. In many Chinese cities, particular streets or districts…

a) change what the shops sell every few months.
b) are allocated to the sale of a particular item.
c) have no shops at all.

3. Western-style convenience stores are not so common in China. What do you find instead?

a) There are only large supermarkets.
b) Rows and rows of shops offering lots of items all in one room.
c) There is only one shop in each city.

4. You can place 'fēngshuǐ' cats in...

a) places that you wish to keep tidy.
b) temples and monasteries.
c) any place where you wish wealth to come.

54 wǔshísì 五十四

Unit 6 – Where?

Saying and writing one in Chinese

The word for 'one', **yī**, changes tone in conversation:
When counting, it is pronounced yī, e.g. **yī, èr, sān, sì**...
When put before a word in the fourth tone, it is pronounced yí, e.g. **yí gè rén**.
When put before any other word, it is pronounced yì.

Exercise 6.1 – Practice writing one in Chinese
Read the short sentences below and complete the examples of **yī** with the correct tone.
Don't worry if you don't know some of the words! We have completed the first one for you.

1. yì zhāng zhǐ
2. yi bàn gè xiǎoshí
3. yi gè lǎoshī
4. shíyi, shí'èr, shísān
5. yi bēi kāfēi
6. yi píng shuǐ

More counting in Chinese

| 两 | liǎng | = | two (when counting) |
| 本 | běn | = | measure word for counting books |

Exercise 6.2 – Bag Count: Numbers review and using reviewing gè
Complete the list below by filling in the blank spaces with either/or the number, **gè**, or the object in Chinese. We have completed an example for you.

① e.g: 1 bag   yí gè bāo

2 bags   liǎng gè bāo
3 bags   sān gè _____
4 bags   sì _____ bāo
5 bags   _____ gè bāo
6 bags   _____ gè bāo
7 bags   qī _____ _____
8 bags   bā gè _____
9 bags   jiǔ _____ _____
10 bags   shí _____ _____

② 5 pens   wǔ gè _____
4 wallets   sān _____ _____
9 friends   _____ gè _____
5 bags   _____ gè _____
2 teachers   _____ gè _____
7 bags   _____ _____ _____
8 pencils   _____ _____ _____
3 ice creams   _____ _____ _____
10 bags   _____ _____ _____
1 ice cream   _____ _____ _____

Exercise 6.3 – With bigger numbers...
Look at the short sentences below and translate them into Chinese. Remember to look out for the new measure word (**běn**). We have completed an example for you.

e.g.	44 batteries	=	sìshísì gè diànchí
1.	29 bags	=	_____
2.	43 books	=	_____
3.	67 wallets	=	_____
4.	99 mobile phones	=	_____

55 wǔshíwǔ 五十五

Unit 6

Exercise 6.4 - Translation
Read the short English sentences and translate them into Chinese in the spaces to the right. Don't forget to use **gè**! We have completed an example for you.

e.g. I have 6 older sisters.   *Wǒ yǒu liù gè jiějie.*

1. He has 5 older brothers.

2. You don't have 3 younger sisters.

3. She doesn't have 2 younger brothers.

4. I have 3 older sisters.

5. You don't have 4 younger sisters.

Exercise 6.5 - Chinese characters and numbers review
Read the numbers (written in pinyin) and write the correct Chinese characters in the boxes below. We have completed an example for you.

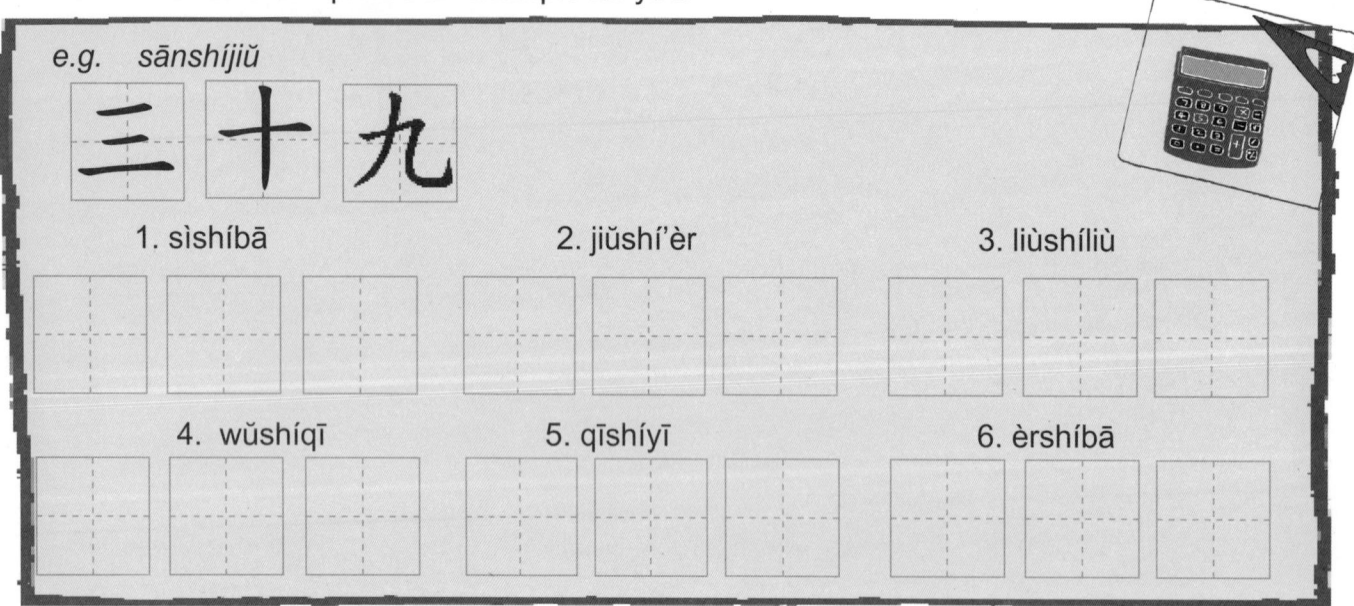

e.g. sānshíjiǔ
三 十 九

1. sìshíbā

2. jiǔshí'èr

3. liùshíliù

4. wǔshíqī

5. qīshíyī

6. èrshíbā

Exercise 6.6 - Translating Chinese characters
Look at the Chinese characters in the sentences below. Write the correct translations for the sentences in English in the gaps provided on the right. We have completed and example for you.

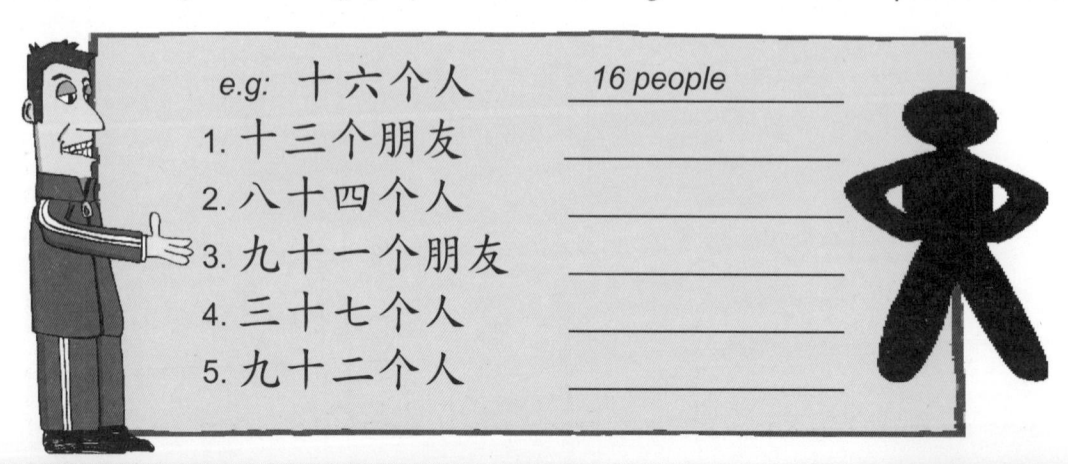

e.g: 十六个人   16 people

1. 十三个朋友

2. 八十四个人

3. 九十一个朋友

4. 三十七个人

5. 九十二个人

56 wǔshíliù 五十六

Unit 6

Exercise 6.7 – More counting
Look at the short sentences written in English below and write them in Chinese characters in the boxes provided. We have completed an example for you.

e.g 5 people

五 个 人

1. 88 friends

2. 48 people

3. 57 people

4. 75 friends

Asking 'how many?'

几   jǐ?   = how many?

A measure word must be used when using **jǐ**.
For example: **jǐ gè bāo?** how many bags?

Exercise 6.8 – How many are there?
Below you will find two lists of English words that you have learnt the meaning for in Chinese. Match these words to the questions on the right. We have completed an example for you.

①
bags	jǐ běn shū?
wallets	jǐ gè bǐ?
older brothers	jǐ gè qiánbāo?
friends	jǐ gè bīngqílín?
newspapers	jǐ gè gēge?
ice creams	jǐ gè péngyou?
pens	*jǐ gè bāo?*
books	jǐ gè bàozhǐ?

②
pencils	jǐ běn kèběn?
people	jǐ gè dìdi?
batteries	jǐ gè jiějie?
older sisters	jǐ gè qiānbǐ?
textbooks	jǐ gè diànchí?
younger sisters	jǐ gè shǒujī?
mobile phones	jǐ gè mèimei?
younger brothers	jǐ gè rén?

57 *wǔshíqī* 五十七

Unit 6

Exercise 6.9 – How many people are there in your family?
Complete the sentences in pinyin for 'How many people are there in your family?' and then count the family members and reply in pinyin in the gaps below. We have completed an example for you.

e.g. Nǐ jiā yǒu jǐ kǒu rén? (How many people are there in your family?) - wǒ - māma - bàba - yí gè gēge *Wǒ jiā yǒu sì kǒu rén.* (There are 4 people in my family)	1. Nǐ jiā yǒu jǐ _____ _____? - wǒ - māma - bàba - liǎng gè gēge _____ _____ yǒu _____ kǒu rén.
2. Nǐ jiā _____ _____ _____ _____? - wǒ - mama - bàba - yí gè jiějie - yí gè gēge - yí gè dìdi Wǒ jiā _____ _____ _____ _____.	3. Nǐ _____ _____ _____ _____ _____? - wǒ - māma - bàba _____ _____ _____ _____ _____ _____.

Exercise 6.10 – Write 'how many' in Chinese characters
First trace over the grey strokes and then complete the <u>full</u> characters <u>3 times</u> in the empty boxes.

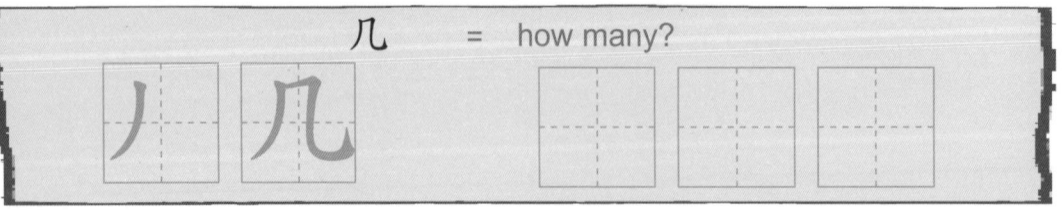

几 = how many?

Exercise 6.11 – Writing 'how many?' in Chinese characters
Read the English sentences and complete the boxes below with the missing Chinese characters. We have completed an example for you.

e.g. How many people?
几 口 人 ?

1. How many younger brothers?
dìdi ?

2. How many older sisters?
jiějie ?

3. How many homes/families?
?

4. How many books?
běn ?

5. How many friends?
?

Unit 6

几口人 jǐ + kǒu + rén?   =   how many people (in a family)?

A special measure word - kǒu - must be used when using jǐ to count the number of people in families.

Exercise 6.12 – Meet their families
Read through the passage and answer the questions in English in the gaps below. We have completed an example for you.

Xiǎoyù: 你好，敏。你好吗？
         Mǐn

Mǐn: 我很好。你家有几口人？
                          jǐ kǒu

Xiǎoyù: 我家有四口人。你呢？
                   kǒu   ne

Mǐn: 我家也有四口人。你有哥哥吗？
                 kǒu   gē ge

Xiǎoyù: 有。他叫小军。你呢？
                    jūn   ne

Mǐn: 也有。他叫明明。
                  Míng ming

Xiǎoyù: 他几岁？

Mǐn: 十四岁。小军呢？
              jūn ne

Xiǎoyù: 他十六岁。

Mǐn: 好。再见。
          Zài jiàn

Xiǎoyù: 再见。
         Zài jiàn

---

e.g. How many people are there in Xiǎoyù's family?   ____Four____

1. How many people are there in Mǐn's family?   _____

2. What is Xiǎoyù's older brother called?   _____

3. Which relative does Mǐn mention? How old is he/she?   _____

4. How old is Xiǎoyù's older brother?   _____

59 wǔshíjiǔ 五十九

Unit 6

How to talk about where things are in Chinese

学校	xuéxiào	= school	在	zài	= to be (located)
动物园	dòngwùyuán	= zoo	你在哪儿	Tā zài nǎr?	= Where are you?
外面	wàimiàn	= outside	我在家	Wǒ zài jiā.	= I am at home.
里面	lǐmian	= inside	他在学校	Tā zài xuéxiào.	= He is at school.

Exercise 6.13 - Look at the clues below and complete the crossword

Complete the crossword below ensuring you use the correct Chinese pinyin for the English clues below. We have completed 1-across for you.

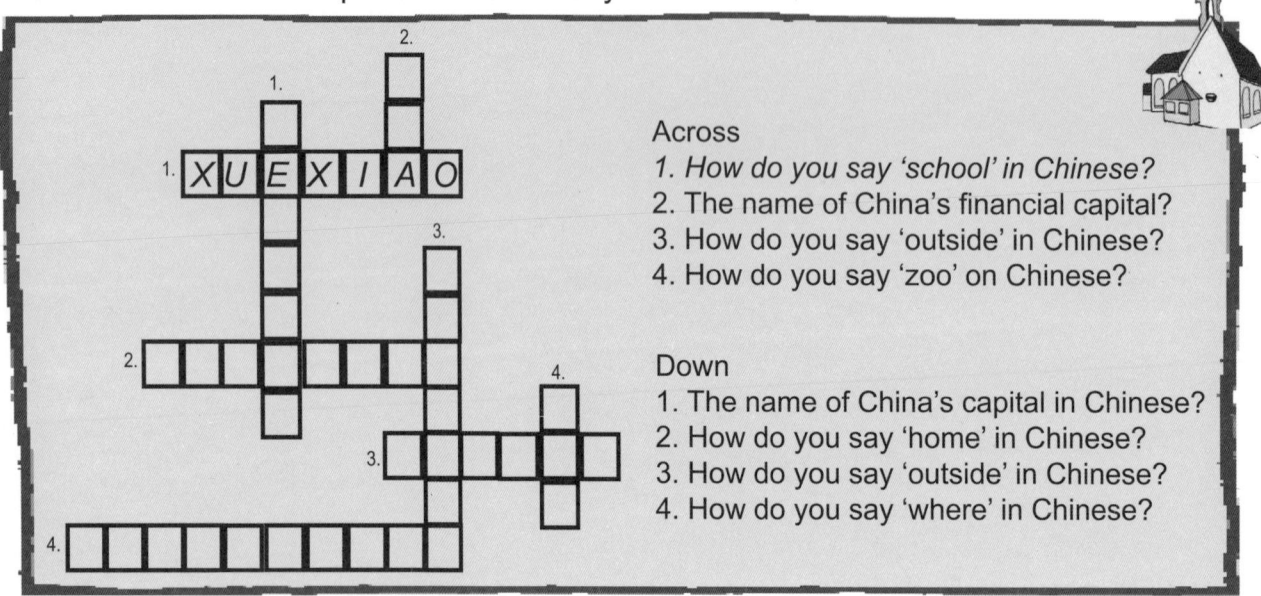

1 across: XUEXIAO

Across
1. How do you say 'school' in Chinese?
2. The name of China's financial capital?
3. How do you say 'outside' in Chinese?
4. How do you say 'zoo' on Chinese?

Down
1. The name of China's capital in Chinese?
2. How do you say 'home' in Chinese?
3. How do you say 'outside' in Chinese?
4. How do you say 'where' in Chinese?

Exercise 6.14 – Where is Katie Reed?

Practise answering the question: Person + **zài nǎr?** Use the crossword in exercise 6.13 to answer the questions below using the structure: **Tā zài** + place. We have completed an example for you.

e.g. Katie zài nǎr? (1 down)   Tā zài Běijīng.

1. Katie zài nǎr? (3 across) _____.
2. Katie zài nǎr? (2 down) _____.
3. Katie zài nǎr? (1 across) _____.
4. Katie zài nǎr? (3 down) _____.

Exercise 6.15 - Translations

Read the English sentences on the left and write the correct translations in Chinese pinyin on the right. We have completed an example for you.

e.g. Where is Dad?   Bàba zài nǎr?

1. Younger brother is at school. _____.
2. Where is younger sister? _____?
3. Older brother is at the zoo. _____.
4. Where is the teacher? _____?
5. Older sister is outside. _____.

60 liùshí 六十

Unit 6

Exercise 6.16 – Writing 'to be (located)' in Chinese characters
First trace over the grey strokes and then complete the full character 3 times in the empty boxes.

在 = to be (located)

Exercise 6.17 – Where are you?
Complete the sentences using the correct Chinese pinyin and characters in the spaces and boxes below. We have completed an example for you.

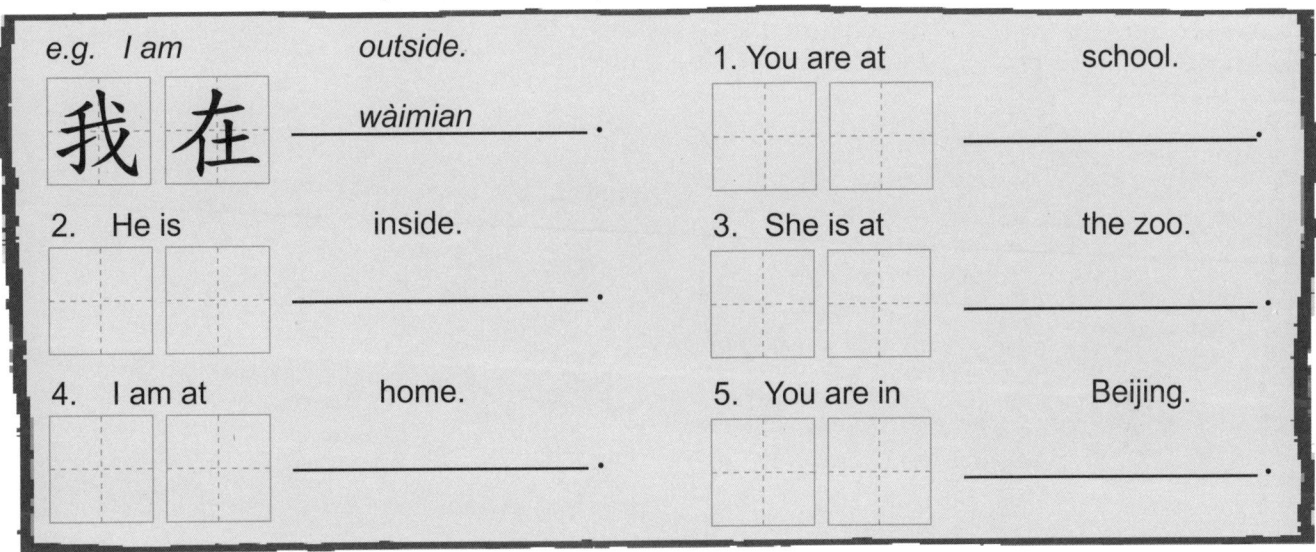

e.g. I am outside.
我 在 _wàimian_.

1. You are at school.

2. He is inside.

3. She is at the zoo.

4. I am at home.

5. You are in Beijing.

Exercise 6.18 – Where are they?
Read through the passage and answer the questions below in English in the gaps to the right. We have completed an example for you.

爸爸	在	哪儿？	他	在	家。	
	zài	nǎr		zài		
姐姐	在	哪儿？	她	在	外面。	
Jiě jie	zài	nǎr		zài	wài miàn	
弟弟	在	哪儿？	他	在	北京。	
Dì di	zài	nǎr		zài	Běi jīng	
妹妹	在	哪儿？	她	在	外面。	
Mèi mei	zài	nǎr		zài	wài miàn	
哥哥	在	哪儿？	他	在	动物园。	
Gē ge	zài	nǎr		zài	dòng wù yuán	
老师	在	哪儿？	他	在	学校。	
Lǎo shī	zài	nǎr		zài	xué xiào	
妈妈	在	哪儿？	她	在	里面。	
	zài	nǎr		zài	lǐ mian	
静	在	哪儿？	她	在	上海。	
Jìng	zài	nǎr		zài	Shàng hǎi	

e.g. Where is older brother?
— He is at the zoo.

1. Where is younger brother?

2. Where is Mum?

3. Where is younger sister?

4. Where is Dad?

5. Where is teacher?

61 liùshíyī 六十一

Unit 6

Positions and furniture

前面	qiánmian	=	in front
后面	hòumian	=	behind
上面	shàngmian	=	on/above
下面	xiàmian	=	below

桌子	zhuōzi	=	table
椅子	yǐzi	=	chair
门	mén	=	door

爸爸在哪儿 Bàba zài nǎr?
Where is dad?

爸爸在桌子下面 Bàba zài zhuōzi xiàmian.
Dad is under the table.

6.19 Picture Link - find the person!
Look at the pictures and link the pictures to the positional phrases written below. We have completed the first one for you.

1. zhuōzi shàngmian
2. mén qiánmian
3. mén hòumian
4. yǐzi qiánmian
5. zhuōzi xiàmian

6.20 Short translations - where is the person?
Look at the short English sentences and write the correct translations in pinyin. We have completed the first one for you.

1. The person is on the chair. — *Rén zài yǐzi shàngmian.*
2. The person is behind the door. — _____.
3. The person is under the the chair. — _____.
4. The person is in front of the table. — _____.

6.21 Writing activity - Fill the gaps
Look at the pictures and complete the gaps below, ensuring that you complete the answers (please choose the correct Chinese word for the <u>family member</u>, the <u>position</u> and the <u>object</u> to which their position relates). We have completed the first one for you.

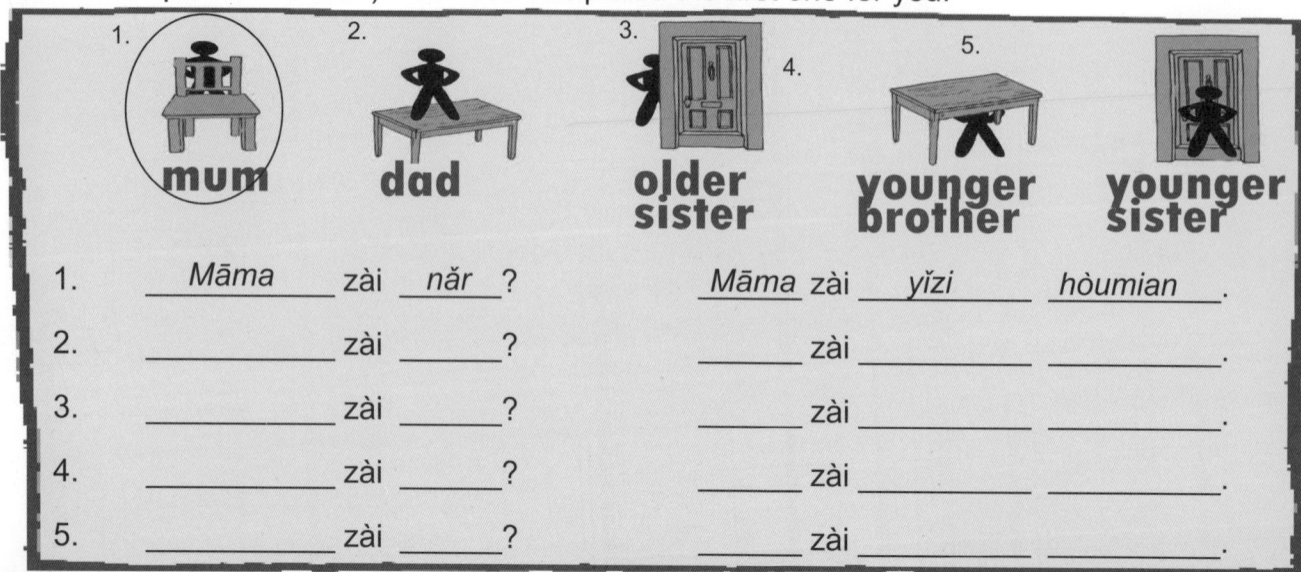

1. mum
2. dad
3. older sister
4. younger brother
5. younger sister

1. *Māma* zài *nǎr* ?   *Māma* zài *yǐzi* *hòumian* .
2. _____ zài _____ ?   _____ zài _____ _____ .
3. _____ zài _____ ?   _____ zài _____ _____ .
4. _____ zài _____ ?   _____ zài _____ _____ .
5. _____ zài _____ ?   _____ zài _____ _____ .

62 liùshí'èr 六十二

Unit 6

Countries of the world

Exercise 6.22 - Countries link
Correctly link the English words on the left to the Chinese words on the right. We have completed the first one for you.

1. America		a.	法国	Fǎguó
2. France		b.	英国	Yīngguó
3. Britain		c.	日本	Rìběn
4. Japan		d.	美国	Měiguó
5. China		e.	中国	Zhōngguó
6. Canada		f.	加拿大	Jiānádà

Exercise 6.23 - Countries search
In the word search below you must find all the countries listed in exercise 6.22. We have completed the first one for you.

x	d	m	f	x	f	j	t
f	f	p	e	k	r	c	k
a	c	q	j	i	q	d	p
g	d	t	b	c	g	j	x
u	k	e	k	x	z	u	p
o	n	x	u	d	a	l	o
c	u	l	o	t	d	f	l
j	q	g	g	k	a	c	p
t	f	l	g	f	n	q	t
l	q	d	n	n	a	d	p
x	t	x	o	k	i	k	x
l	p	j	h	p	j	y	k
c	x	c	z	t	c	f	j

City living

北京	Běijīng	=	Beijing
伦敦	Lúndūn	=	London
纽约	Niǔ Yuē	=	New York
巴黎	Bālí	=	Paris

你住在那儿 Nǐ zhù zài nǎr?
Where do you live?

我住在伦敦 Wǒ zhù zài Lúndūn.
I live in London.

Exercise 6.24 - Where do you live?
Answer each of the questions below using the correct subject pronoun + **zhù zài** + country/city. We have completed an example for you.

e.g. Nǐ zhù zài nǎr? (Beijing)   Wǒ zhù zài Běijīng.
1. Nǐ zhù zài nǎr? (London)   _____.
2. Tā zhù zài nǎr? (New York)   _____.
3. Nǐ zhù zài nǎr? (Japan)   _____.
4. Tā zhù zài nǎr? (Paris)   _____.

63 liùshísān 六十三

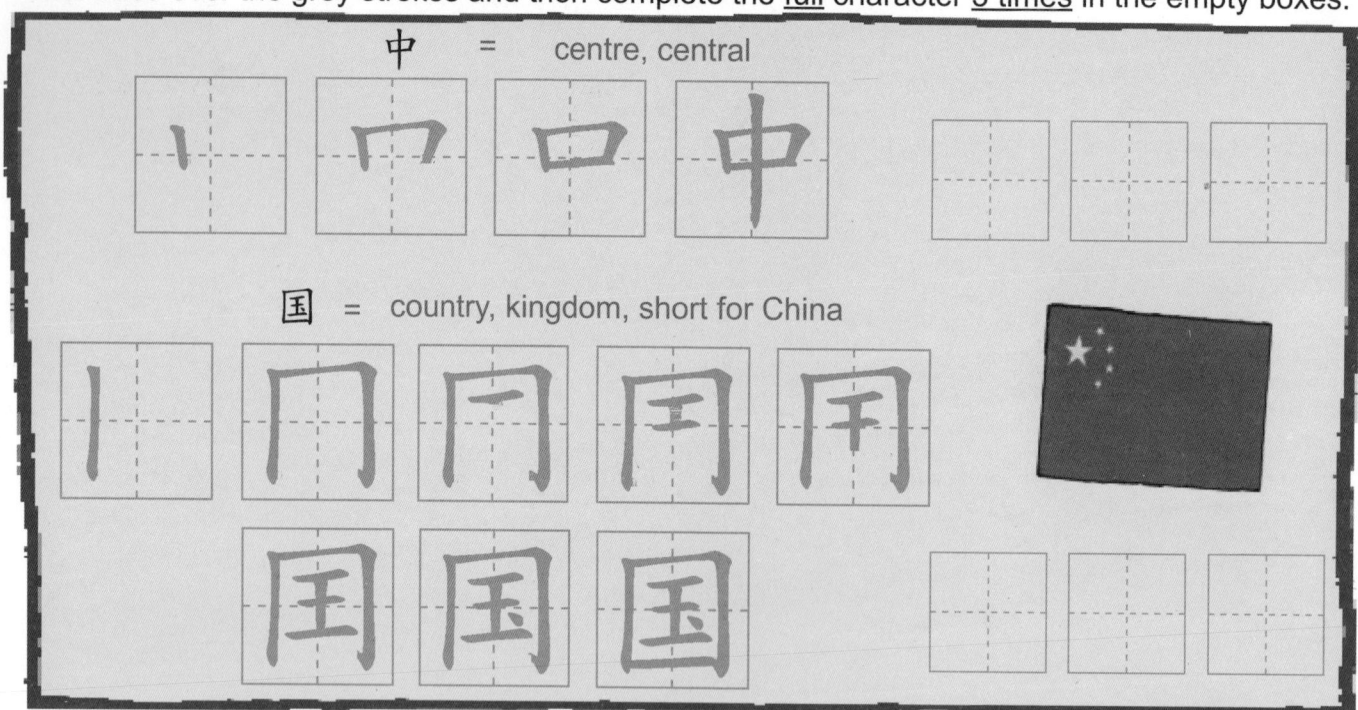

Unit 6

Exercise 6.25 - Practise writing 'China' in Chinese characters
First trace over the grey strokes and then complete the full character 3 times in the empty boxes.

中 = centre, central

国 = country, kingdom, short for China

Exercise 6.26 - Practise writing 'Britain' in Chinese characters
First trace over the grey strokes and then complete the full character 3 times in the empty boxes.

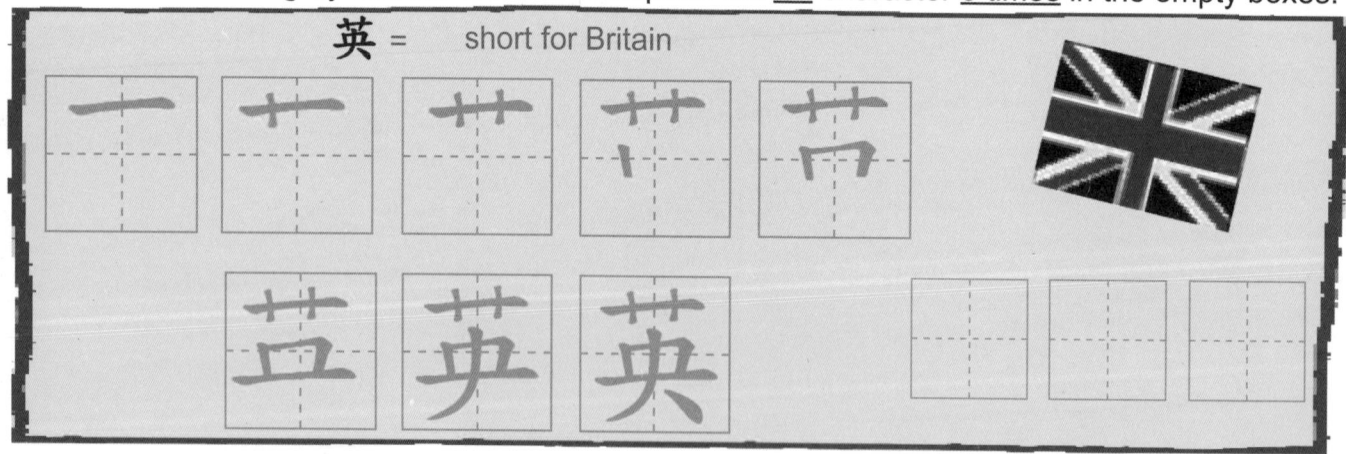

英 = short for Britain

Exercise 6.27 - Reading comprehension
Read through the passage below and answer the questions in English in the spaces provided. We have completed the first one for you.

你好。我 叫 芳芳。我 十二 岁。我 住 在 中 国, 北 京。
　　　　　jiào Fāng fang　　　　　　　　　　　　 zhù zài Zhōng guó Běi jīng

我 家 有 四 口 人。我 爸爸 妈妈 也 住 在 北京。
　　　　　　kǒu　　　　　　　　　　　 zhù zài Běi jīng

我 有 姐 姐 - 她 叫 静。她 十七 岁. 她 住 在 英 国, 伦 敦。
　　 jiě jie　　　 jiào Jìng　　　　　　　　　 zhù zài Yīng guó Lún dūn

1. What is the subject called?　　　_Fāngfang_
2. How old is she?　　　_____
3. How many people are there in her family?　_____
4. Who lives in London?　_____

64 liùshísì 六十四

Unit 6

Which nationality are you?

Structure: **Nǐ** + **shì** + **nǎ guó** + **rén**.	Structure: Person + **shì** + country + **rén**.
你是哪国人 Nǐ shì nǎ guó rén? = Which nationality are you?	我是英国人 Wǒ shì Yīngguórén. = I am British.

Exercise 6.28 – Which nationality are you?
Answer each of the questions below using the correct country and subject pronoun (I/ you/ he/ she). We have completed an example for you.

e.g. Nǐ shì nǎ guó rén? (Britain)   Wǒ shì Yīngguórén.

1. Nǐ shì nǎ guó rén?   (America)   _____.
2. Tā shì nǎ guó rén?   (Japan)   _____.
3. Tā shì nǎ guó rén?   (Canada)   _____.
4. Nǐ shì nǎ guó rén?   (France)   _____.

Exercise 6.29 – Ask and answer the question
Complete the sentences on the right according to the structure which has been explained in the guide at the top. To answer the questions, use **tā**. We have completed the first one for you.

e.g. David Beckham?   David Beckham shì nǎ guó rén? Tā shì Yīngguórén.

1. Thierry Henry?   _____.
2. Tiger Woods?   _____.
3. Jackie Chan?   _____.
4. A ninja?   _____.

Exercise 6.30 – About our friends
Read through the passage below and answer the questions in English in the spaces provided. We have completed the first one for you.

Katie 的 朋友 叫 小军。 他 是 中 国 人。 他 住 在 中 国。
                    jūn   Zhōng guó   zhù zài Zhōng guó

明 明 的 朋友 叫 John。 他 是 加拿大人。 他住 在 美国。
Míng ming   jiào   Jiā ná dà   zhù zài Měi guó

静 的 朋友 叫 Mika – 她 是 日本人。 她 住 在 法 国。
Jìng   jiào   Rì běn   zhù zài Fǎ guó

1. Where does Xiǎojūn live?   _China_____
2. What nationality is Míngming's friend? _____
3. Where does Míngming's friend live?   _____
4. Where does Mika live?   _____

65 liùshíwǔ 六十五

Unit 6

The Plural in Chinese

我们	Wǒ<u>men</u>	=	We
你们	Nǐ<u>men</u>	=	You (plural)
他们	Tā<u>men</u>	=	They, them (masculne)
她们	Tā<u>men</u>	=	They, them (feminine)

Exercise 6.31 – Translation: practise writing the plurals

Read the short English sentences and translate them into Chinese pinyin in the spaces to the right. We have completed an example for you.

e.g. We are British. → Wǒmen shì Yīngguórén.

1. They (feminine) live in France. _____.

2. We are at school. _____.

3. You (plural) are Chinese. _____.

4. They (masculine) are behind the chair. _____.

Exercise 6.32 – More 'plural' practice

Create the correct link between the Chinese pinyin on the left and the English sentences on the right. We have completed an example for you.

1. Tāmen shì Fǎguórén ma?   a. You (plural) live in London.
2. Nǐmen zài mén qiánmian.   b. We have three bags.
3. Wǒmen yǒu sān gè bāo.   c. They are Japanese.
4. Tāmen shì Rìběnren.   d. We don't have water.
5. Nǐmen zhù zài Lúndūn.   e. Are they French?
6. Wǒmen méiyǒu shuǐ.   f. You (plural) are in front of the door.

Exercise 6.33 – Writing the plural marker (-men) in Chinese characters

First trace over the grey strokes and then complete the full character 3 times in the empty boxes.

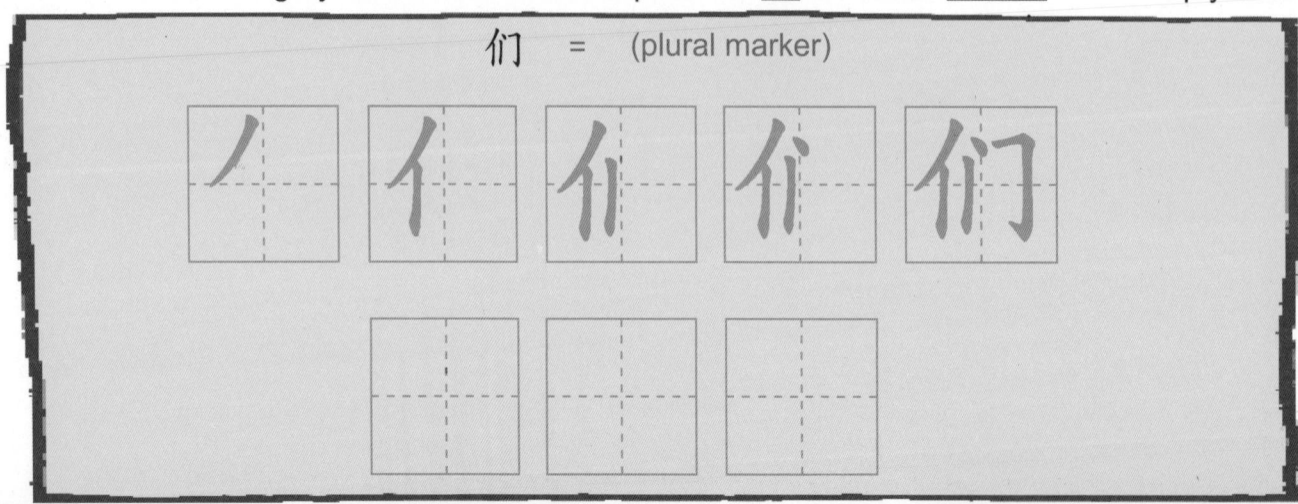

们 = (plural marker)

66 liùshíliù 六十六

Unit 6

Exercise 6.34 – Reading comprehension
Read through the 3 short passages below and answer the questions in English. We have completed an example for you.

我 叫 之霖。 我 五十一 岁。 我 家 有 四 口 人 – 我 们
    jiào Zhī lín   kǒu   men

住 在 中 国, 北 京。
zhù zài Zhōng guó Běi jīng

我 叫 国 英。我 十五 岁。我 有 妹 妹。她 叫 马丽,她 八 岁
    jiào Guó yīng   mèi mei   jiào   lì

– 我们 住 在 日本。
    men zhù zài Rì běn

我 叫 阳阳。 我 有 两 个 朋友。 他们 是 美国人– 他们 住 在
    jiào Yáng yang   liǎng   Měi guó   men zhù zài

法国, 巴黎。
Fǎ guó Bā lí

e.g. How old is Zhīlín ?	51 years old
1. How many people are there in his family?	
2. Where do Guóyīng and his sister live?	
3. What nationality are Yángyang's friends?	
4. Which city do they live in?	

Silk in Chinese

One of the most important Chinese exports, silk gave its name to a trading route that crosses the whole of Asia: the Silk Road. Silk also has its own character element, 纟, which is a simplified picture of a twisted thread.

Exercise 6.35 – Practise writing 'silk' in Chinese characters.
First trace over the grey strokes and then complete the <u>full</u> character <u>3 times</u> in the empty boxes.

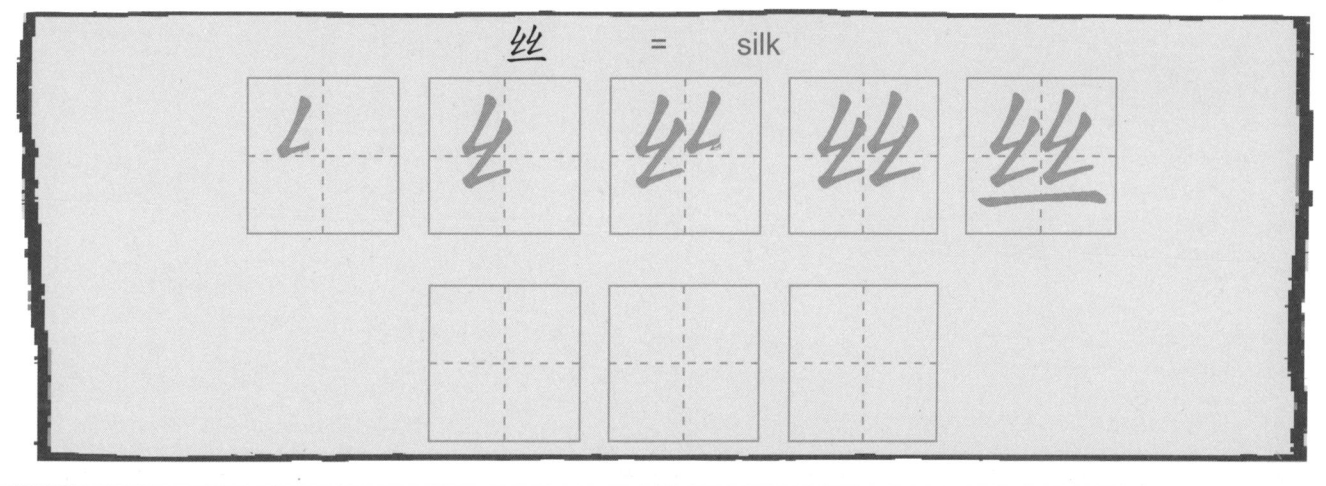

丝 = silk

Unit 6

Chinese New Year

Exercise 6.36 – What did you learn? Question time!

e.g. If you go to China during Chinese New Year, you will most likely hear the sound of:
- quiet talking ☐
- people arguing ☐
- fireworks everywhere ☑

1. What is the name of the legendary beast, most prominent at Chinese Year.
   - Nián ☐
   - Niān ☐
   - Miàn ☐

2. In China, red is the colour of: Happiness and _____?

3. What are the name of the red envelopes that are given to children at Chinese New Year?
   - Hóng bǎn ☐
   - Hóng bāo ☐
   - Háng bāo ☐

4. What are **jiǎozi**? _____

Chinese Signs of the Zodiac

Exercise 6.37 – Write your animal in Chinese!

Below is a list of the different animals that are celebrated for the Chinese New Year. You can see which year is associated with which animal and the cycle of animals i.e. 2020 will be the Year of the Rat, 2021 the Year of the Ox and so on. Using this 12-year cycle, you can count back the years to find out which 'animal was being celebrated' and thus what 'year' people were when they were born. <u>Write your and your family's animal years in Chinese!</u>

Zodiac Animal	Year	Zodiac Animal	Year
鼠 – Rat	2008	马 – Horse	2014
牛 – Ox	2009	羊 – Sheep / Goat	2015
虎 – Tiger	2010	猴 – Monkey	2016
兔 – Rabbit	2011	鸡 – Chicken	2017
龙 – Dragon	2012	狗 – Dog	2018
蛇 – Snake	2013	猪 – Pig	2019

Your animal   Your family members